MW00814924

Sword of Love

The Travail of Pakistan and Bangladesh

Gwen Shaw

Engeltal Press
P.O. Box 447
Jasper, ARK 72641
(870) 446-2665
www.EngeltalPress.com

Engeltal Press
P.O. Box 447
Jasper, ARK 72641
(870) 446-2665
www.EngeltalPress.com

ISBN: 0-9759327-5-6
ISBN13: 978-0-9759327-5-9

The following story is true. The events are told as they actually happened.

The names of many of the people and towns we visited were deliberately left out or changed. This was done to protect these people from recrimination.

Printed in the United States of America

P 146 Chris

DEDICATION

*This book is dedicated to
the people of Bangladesh and Pakistan
with the prayers
that God's blessing will shine upon them both.*

FOREWORD

We have brought this fascinating true story of our high adventures in Pakistan and Bangladesh out of the archives because Pakistan is playing a very important role in today's news, and many do not know the true story of the history of Pakistan.

We were there when it happened. We have preached the Gospel to the parents of today's Taliban. We have seen God do miracles, signs and wonders among the people whose sons we are fighting today.

John Osteen, the father of Joel Osteen, told me, "Sister Gwen, your book, *Sword of Love*, is the greatest missionary book I have ever read."

Much has happened since we walked those streets, preached in those mountains and cities, in churches, halls, tents, and even under the open sky. Many who lived and worked with us are no longer among us—they have gone on to their eternal reward. Many who heard us preach have gone into eternity, some to Heaven and some who listened to us tell the story of God's love, but refused His Son, Jesus... lost forever. But we did what we could, and we paid the price long ago.

With this edition, we pass the torch on to you, this new generation. We beg you, "Do not kill tomorrow's harvest field!"

The gift of the Bible to your enemy is better than the "gift" of a bullet!

Jesus commanded us to love our enemy. Love is the most powerful weapon we have. It will disarm our enemy.

Gwen R. Shaw, 2009

INTRODUCTION

"I thought I would ask of Thee — but I dared not — the rose wreath Thou hadst on Thy neck. Thus I waited for the morning, when Thou didst depart, to find a few fragments on the bed. And like a beggar, I searched the dawn only for a stray petal or two.

"Ah me, what is it I find? What token left of Thy love? It is no flower, no spices, no vase of perfumed water. It is Thy mighty SWORD, flashing as a flame, heavy as a bolt of thunder. The young light of morning comes through the window and spreads itself upon Thy bed. The morning bird twitters and asks, 'Woman, what hast thou got?'

"No, it is no flower, nor spices, nor vase of perfumed water; it is Thy dreadful SWORD.

"I sit and muse in wonder, what gift is this of Thine? I can find no place where to hide it. I am ashamed to wear it, frail as I am, and it hurts me when I press it to my bosom. Yet shall I bear in my heart this honour of the burden of pain, this gift of Thine.

"From now there shall be no fear left for me in this world, and Thou shalt be victorious in all Thy strife. Thou hast left death for my companion, and I shall crown him with my life. Thy SWORD is with me to cut asunder my bonds, and there shall be no fear left for me in the world.

"From now I leave off all petty decorations. Lord of my heart, no more shall there be for me waiting and weeping in corners, no more coyness and sweetness of demeanour. Thou has given me Thy SWORD for adornment. No more doll's decorations for me!"

Rabindranath Tagore

Out of Bengal come the writings of Bengali's greatest poet. By divine revelation he sees the great eternal truth which few men dare to see, that the sword is but our friend to set us gloriously free.

Without the sword that pierced Mary's heart, we would all be in bondage today. But the sword that gave her pain has given us liberty. Perhaps this is why the Master said, "I came not to send peace, but the sword!"

How wonderful that God does take this vicious looking instrument of war and death, and wielding it, brings peace and life. Yes! And also liberty!

The strange thing is that often the sword that cuts the deepest is the one that is held in the hand of a brother or a neighbour. Let us not hate the one whom God uses to bring this sword of separation and pain into our lives. Let us accept it; and what is more, let us press it to our bosom with pride, for it is a great honour for a man or a nation when the great and dreadful sword cuts off that which we hold dear. For in the pain and through the tears, we must see that the hand that held it was not the one we supposed it to be, but that of God.

All other ornamentation is cheap, when compared to the costly sword of love, held in the Hand of the One Who is Love.

I have tried to tell the story of Pakistan and Bangladesh not only as it was told to me, but also as we experienced it. It may not be perfect, or complete. I have told it without personal prejudice to either country, for I love both equally. Many things about the year of sorrow and suffering I do not understand myself, nor how a people as beautiful as those of West Pakistan could perform acts so cruel and heartless. I pray that when the mist is cleared and the tears are dried away, Bangladesh will be able to accept the sword of tragedy as a SWORD OF LOVE, and in doing so, be truly FREE.

SWORD OF LOVE

GLOSSARY

1. Burka — a covering, resembling a veil, worn by Muslim women. It can be white or black or another dark colour, and can be either waist-length or longer.

2. John 20:24, 25. Thomas could not believe that Jesus was risen from the dead until he used his natural senses of sight and touch.

3. I Corinthians 14:34.

4. Memsahiba — a polite term for "madam" applying particularly to foreign ladies.

5. Genesis 4:9.

6. One crore equals ten million.

7. India said in August 1973 that she was releasing the 93,000 Pakistani prisoners of war.

Part One

STORM CLOUDS

Sigi, Betty, and I were sitting around the breakfast table in Karachi, West Pakistan. We were enjoying our second cup of coffee when suddenly Betty's husband, Mark, turned the radio on to listen to the news. There had been violent riots the last two days in Karachi, and, in fact, that was the reason we were at the Smith's home. "Perhaps," said Mark, "Radio Pakistan will tell us a little of the news."

"Police report that six were killed yesterday in the rioting that broke out in the center of the city at 9:00 a.m. Over a hundred have been arrested." We knew the report was not true. We had been in the midst of it and had seen the violence of the mob gone mad. The gross understatement was given purposely, so that the public would not be disturbed by the truth.

Suddenly our attention was drawn to a new announcement from Dacca, in East Pakistan. "The foreign embassies in East Pakistan have advised their nationals to leave at once. Intense rioting and fighting has broken out in some parts but the West Pakistan soldiers have now been ordered to the scenes of disturbance and they have the situation well in hand. All is peaceful in East Pakistan and business is proceeding as usual."

As Mark left for his day's work we three looked at each other. We knew that we were only hearing a small portion of the truth. My heart was filled with anxiety for the many Americans, Germans, British, and others who were now faced with the sudden decision to obey their government's advice and depart, thus leaving behind a lifetime of friends and work, or to stay and take the consequences.

This was 1971, and terrible events were developing. How

helpless we three women felt! How useless in a world crisis! What could we do in the face of suffering and death?

"Oh, let us pray!" I said, as the pain of others gripped around my heart and claimed it as its own. Together we called upon our Heavenly Father to go to East Pakistan and help a people who were in the agony of a great political crisis. Suddenly I knew that Sigi had to go – God was sending her to East Pakistan.

"Speak the Word of Prophecy," the Spirit whispered to me, "and tell her I will send her."

I looked at this lovely young woman who had already endured an age of suffering under the hardship of East Berlin's Communism, and I said, "No, Lord, I cannot tell her she must go into death and danger. Please do not ask such a thing of me. If you want her to go, You tell her Yourself."

After praying, we wiped our tears and, excusing ourselves, Sigi and I went into our room to get ready to go out. Suddenly Sigi sat down and said, "Gwen, I don't know how you will take this, but I have to go to East Pakistan. God spoke to me as we were praying. I asked Him to confirm it to me through a prophecy from you, but even though He didn't, I have to tell you. I must go. Please try to understand." She looked at me, her appealing brown eyes full of tears.

I was standing at the dresser, my back to her. I turned and looked at her as she was speaking. "I know. God showed me you must go. He even gave me a message to give you, but I wouldn't do it. I just couldn't – I didn't want to be responsible for your death."

"Oh Gwen, thank God He spoke to you. I didn't know how to tell you, I was afraid you would think I had gone mad."

"No, Sigi, you are not mad. It is God," I answered. "But when do you think you should go? We have just arrived a week ago and everywhere our meetings have been announced. People are expecting us."

"I will finish our meetings here, and then I will go when you return to America."

"Good," I said. Little did either of us realize the effect of this commitment to each other and to God.

"COME TO PAKISTAN"

For a number of years the invitation to come to Pakistan had been extended to me. People there had heard of my ministry in India and had begun to pray, "God, send Sister Gwen to us." Over and over I had to say no to their invitations. It wasn't God's time – I did not feel called yet.

Finally, after Sigi and I returned from our trip behind the Iron Curtain and I was in the midst of writing the book **Sigi and I**, God suddenly spoke and said, "Write Naseem Raza, My servant in Karachi, West Pakistan, and tell him you are coming."

At that time I was not well. I was physically exhausted, and it looked like a fool's deed to write and say, "I'm coming to Pakistan." Nevertheless, I knew God had spoken.

As I knelt by my bed and prayed, my one desire was, "Oh God, give me Your love and burden for the land." I have always asked God to love through me each nation to which He sends me. I will go any place He wants on one condition – that I go with God's love in my heart. Without that, I had better stay at home.

For years I had loved India, and Pakistan was only a name. What's more, it was the name of an enemy of my beloved India. In the previous 24 years since the partition in 1947 and the birth of Pakistan, the two countries had had many skirmishes at the border and one war which had been stopped. Now these two brothers were living in a temporary and suspicious truce, which could erupt at any moment into a war which could involve the whole world.

God had spoken to Pakistan, for everywhere people spoke with fear and apprehension of the strange sign which had for several nights been seen by multitudes in the Pakistan sky. In hushed tones people told how a strange dagger had hung visibly in the sky over Pakistan, as though held by an invisible hand. It was at that time that Zulfikar Ali Bhutto, the man of mystery and strength, had come suddenly into power as the new Prime Minister. Pakistan was a nation divided into two parts by a thousand miles of India. In the East were the romantic and temperamental Bengalis, who were predominantly Hindu. In the West were the Punjabi warriors, predominantly Muslim. The nation was not only separated by distance, but by race, religion, and political differences. Sheik Mujibur Rehman, the leader of the people in East Pakistan had openly declared, before thousands, "I am willing to go to prison and to death for my country and my people." The sympathy of India was with East Pakistan.

In addition to these problems, East Pakistan had just that year suffered the world's greatest tidal flood which swept multitudes of helpless people and livestock into the sea. The true number of lives lost has never been fully realized. The world was still talking in shocked sympathy about "Poor East Pakistan." Suddenly this little-known nation was gaining world fame as she began the second half of her dark night of travail and agony.

This was the Pakistan to which God was sending me. Daily the burden of this needy land lay on my heart as I prepared to go.

One morning at 8:00 a.m. the telephone rang. When I picked up the receiver I heard a friend's voice saying, "Sister Gwen, God has given me a vision which concerns you and I feel I must tell you." And then she began to tell how she had seen Jesus walking through a great harvest field which reached as far as the eyes could see. It was harvest time and there was no one to bring in the harvest. Jesus turned and looked so sad, and asked, "Who will go?" And someone in the distance spoke my name, "Sister Gwen." It was repeated so forcibly that she felt she must tell me about it.

"Sister," she said, "I don't know what it means but I had to tell you." I knew what it meant. To me it was confirmation from the Lord that He needed me in one of His great Harvest Fields – Pakistan.

"I WILL SHOW YOU A SIGN"

On my way to Pakistan I stopped in Germany, and was joined by Sigi. God had miraculously made a way for her to join me.

We landed in Delhi, India, and were prevailed upon by friends to stay and work with them for a short while. Now this time was over and we were booked to fly from Delhi to Karachi. We were unable to notify anyone that we were coming because there was no communication between India and Pakistan.

Early on the morning of our departure, while I was praying, God spoke to me and said, "My daughter, you are in My perfect will. As a sign to you, I will give you a special token today." I wondered what this token would be. All day as we were about our business in Delhi, I was looking for God's promise to be fulfilled.

Finally at 10:00 p.m. we went out to Palam Airport, New Delhi, to catch our flight to Karachi, West Pakistan. Enroute there, we were a little anxious about where we should stay when landing in Karachi and how we would contact Naseem Raza and the people there with whom we would work. The city was strange to us. Neither of us had ever been there before.

The plane landed in Karachi, and we passed through immigrations and customs without any difficulty. As we stepped out into the dark night, about two o'clock in the morning, a tall Pakistani walked up to me and asked, "Are you Sister Gwen?"

In surprise I answered, "Yes, I am Sister Gwen."

"I'm Naseem Raza," came the reply.

"Brother," I gasped in surprise, "How did you know to come and meet us on this flight?"

"I was way over on the other side of town, when God spoke to me and said, "They are coming on this flight. Go out to the airport and meet them. So I came."

Suddenly, I knew THIS was the token of the Lord – this

seal of approval which God had promised me. My heart was lifted in joy. Oh God, How Great Thou Art!

"WE'LL ALL
BE DEAD BY EVENING"

The following day we started our meetings in the Methodist church — teaching Christian doctrine, and healing the sick. The crowds were increasing until there were almost as many outside the church as could get inside.

Sigi and I were staying at the Y.W.C.A. building in the heart of Karachi. One morning early, Sigi was awakened by a strange noise. Quietly, she got up, and slipped out of the room to see what was happening. I awoke as she excitedly entered the room, "Gwen, there's a riot or something on the street. There are big crowds of people, screaming and yelling, and they are turning cars upside down and setting them on fire. Come and see!"

Quickly, I got into my clothes, and together we climbed the steps to the second balcony. Chaos was everywhere. People seemed to have gone mad. The screaming of the mobs sounded worse than wild animals. Everywhere there were fires, as cars were being burned up by the mobs.

We went to look for some of the other women of the hostel. There they were, hiding behind a lattice on the second floor, watching with fear the scene of confusion and hate on the street below. The building beside us was already on fire and the fire engines couldn't get through the mobs to put it out.

The secretary of the hostel was sitting in a cold sweat. Someone had brought her heart pills. "Oh dear God," she cried, "we'll all be dead by evening."

I put my hand on her shoulder gently and said, "No, we won't, for the angels of the Lord are with us to protect us." I spoke with confidence because I knew many at home were praying for us, and surely God would protect us.

"If only those madmen don't climb over the wall . . . ,"

someone said.

"If they do, God alone knows what will happen to us."

The gate was closed and barred, and the wall was quite strong and high, but not so high that it was impossible to scale it. For a time we watched the increasing fury of the mobs. Someone was screaming through a loudspeaker, "Down with the Imperialists! Down with the Government!"

Just then, some men began climbing over the wall into our compound. When others saw it, they did the same thing. We saw crowds of wild and angry men swiftly gaining entry into our yard.

Quickly, Sigi and I went to our room on the ground floor. We ran inside, and locking the door behind us, knelt down to pray. We expected someone to bang on our door, demanding entrance, but after some time, when no one came, and we heard nothing, we went out to see what had happened. Much to our amazement, we saw that God had "taken the fight" out of the men. They were sitting calmly under the trees and "cooling off." We had to smile. God still could turn lions into lambs.

We looked at our watches. It was time to start getting ready for the evening meeting. It seemed it would be impossible for us to go. We couldn't even get out of the gate. But, believing, we began to get ready. Finally, we were dressed in our white saris, and came downstairs. The gateman opened the gate especially for us, and we stepped out on the street, where minutes before had been hate, killings and violence. All was quiet. There was hardly a soul in sight.

"Where will we find a taxi?" Sigi asked.

We had many miles to go, and without a means of conveyance, we could never get to the meeting. All day long there hadn't been a taxi near the place.

We stood for a moment and prayed, "Father, You know we need to get to the meeting tonight. Please send a taxi for Your daughters."

Around the corner came the first taxi of the day, and we flagged it down. Within minutes of coming out of the gate, we were on our way to the meeting.

BLESSED WATER

That night our meeting was out in a village amongst a settlement of low-caste people, or sweepers, as they are known.

As we entered that simple village of huts, and found our way by torch and kerosene lamp to the place where the meeting was, I saw the crowd had gathered. When we were seated on the make-shift "platform," I looked at the table in front of us which was to be our lectern. There must have been over forty cups, glasses, and bottles of water on it.

Now, quite often I like a little sip of water when I am speaking, but this was certainly far more than I would need in a month. "Do they expect us to drink that much water?" I asked in amazement.

Sigi suggested that we better drink some of it, as a token of appreciation for their kindness to us in supplying us with a drink. She drank some, and I did too, but there still were about forty glasses of water left.

Finally, my curiosity got the best of me. I turned to my interpreter and asked, "Why did they bring us so much water? Are we supposed to drink it all?"

"No, sister," he answered. "These are only brought by the people, so you will bless the water, and then they will sprinkle it in their homes to drive out evil spirits, and give it to their sick to heal them."

I thought about Acts 19:11, 12 where something like this is recorded in the Apostle Paul's ministry. "And God gave Paul the power to do unusual miracles, so that even when his handkerchiefs or parts of his clothing were placed upon sick people, they were healed, and any demons within them came out." (Living Bible)

"So what," I said to myself, "if these people were too poor to afford oil, and had to make do with water, could God not work the same miracles with water, as with oil?"

So we blessed the water in the Name of Jesus, and the people carried their vessels home with joy.

"GWEN, YOU'VE GOT TO COME
AND SEE WHAT'S GOING ON!"

That night, when we returned to the city, we stopped at the Intercontinental Hotel for a milkshake. Suddenly I said to Sigi, "Let's phone my brother and ask him and his wife to come and have a little fellowship with us." My brother Earl and his wife had arrived in Karachi that week and were sharing with us in the meetings.

When I got them on the phone, he said, "Oh Gwen, you've got to come and see what is going on here on the streets outside our hotel."

Immediately we rushed over. The taxi driver refused to drive up to the hotel because the street was packed full of thousands of people. So we got out and began pushing our way through the crowd. All of them were men, for Muslim women do not move about much on the streets. A drum was beating and wild music was playing, working the mob into a frenzy. Quickly we squeezed our way through, and climbed up the four flights of stairs to the room.

There, from the verandah, we watched the scene of religious fanaticism below. At the heights of excitement, fiery coals were strewn out over the street, and men walked through them, barefoot.

Suddenly, we heard the sharp crack of a whip. And to our utter horror, we saw men lashing the bare limbs of others with the cruel stroke of a bull whip. We watched, as men walked deliberately into the pathway of the man wielding the whip. It seemed as if they had a certain kind of pride at the scar of bleeding, torn flesh, which the whiplash left across their bodies and limbs.

We watched this scene until midnight, with unbelieving eyes. And finally as the streets began to clear we walked back to our hostel. We looked like two angels in white as we passed through the streets. People stared at us.

Suddenly, out of the dark, a young man walked up to us and said in English, "It is dangerous for two ladies to walk on the streets alone on a night like this. Let me escort you to wherever you are going."

We didn't feel we needed him; we had the angels. But then, he had offered out of the kindness of his heart, and we couldn't refuse him, so he walked us to our gate, where he left us. We never saw him again.

"THERE WILL BE TWO PAKISTANS"

A strange thing happened one night while I was preaching. It was while we still were holding meetings at the Methodist church. I was speaking about the signs of the end-time, reiterating the hate which was filling men's hearts everywhere, and telling how there was a separation everywhere, amongst friends, in homes, in churches, in denominations, in business organizations, and even in nations.

"There are two Koreas," I said, "two Chinas, two Vietnams, two Germanys, even two Berlins. There are two Canadas, the French- and the English-speaking; two Americas, the black and the white; two Indias; and last of all there shall be two Pakistans."

It wasn't until these prophetic words had been loudly proclaimed from my own lips that I realized what had been spoken. It was not of my own self, but the Holy Spirit of God had spoken in foreknowledge through my mouth. Little did we realize that before the year was out, we would see the fulfillment of these words, with the winning of a terrible conflict, and the proclamation of a new nation − Bangladesh!

"YOU MUST GET OUT OF THERE"

The day following the riots, Sigi and I were invited for dinner at the home of Betty and Mark Smith, who are missionaries from Canada. After the meagre fare of the last few days, we were very happy to accept. The Smiths were very anxious for our welfare. The radio had warned that there would be further rioting that day in the same area where we lived. Certain elements were angry because of the ones who had been killed the day before.

"You must get out of there," they said. "It's too dangerous for you to stay. When the mobs go mad, anything can happen. Please come and stay with us." And so it was that we decided to come and stay with the Smiths until the next day, when we would be leaving Karachi to continue meetings somewhere else.

The news warned us that the riots would begin at 2:00 p.m. It was now 1:30. "Hurry," said Betty, "or you will never make it. Mark will help you."

We jumped in their car and hurried to our hostel. Already the mobs were gathering. All around us we could hear the ominous sound of threatening crowds. It sounded like an approaching herd of wild buffalo. The gateman was just preparing to lock the outer gate. The secretary, and other women were nervous and fearful. Quickly, we paid our bill and dashed into our room to pack. Mark had said, "Make it quick, girls. I'll give you ten minutes."

Unfortunately, both Sigi and I are the kind who scatter everything about the place. We looked frantically about our room. Cosmetics on the two dressing tables, clothes in the closet, stuff in drawers, books and papers under both beds, shoes in odd corners, and toiletries in the bathroom. We dashed around like two wild women, throwing things into cases and bags. At the door stood the porter, hurrying us to give him the bags, so he could carry them to the car.

"Hurry girls," shouted Mark. "They are getting closer, and these people want to shut the gates."

The roar of the mob was getting louder. It fairly curdled our blood to listen to it.

"Sigi, here, do you have any more room in your case for this?"

"No. Mine is so full now, I can't close it."

"Sit on it. It's got to close."

"What will we do with all these things?"

"Take them as they are."

Finally we started clearing out the room. By this time the porter was assisted by another man who was running back and forth, throwing things in the car, in the trunk, on the roof. We finally got all our stuff together, and into the car, including ourselves. The ladies waved us goodbye with relief. It's always more dangerous to have "foreigners" around. Especially Americans, or anyone with a white face, because the mobs kill you first and find out later what you are. And these women here at the hostel were not too sure that our angels would protect them again. It was better to get rid of us.

The gateman had waited long enough. "Hurry! Hurry!" he was calling impatiently.

Mark started the car, shifted the gears, and away we went! I looked back to see the gateman running after us. In the rush, we had forgotten something on the car top, and it had fallen off. We stopped to retrieve it. This time, as I looked back, I saw the gateman locking the gate with a sigh of relief, and a shake of the head. I knew what he was thinking – "Women!"

"YOU MUST COME TO MY CITY"

Looking at the audience that night in Hyderbad, Pakistan, I saw a woman who was different from all the others. There was such a look of sincerity on her face. I knew, as I gazed down on her, watching her worshipping the Lord, that she had a deep love for God, and lived in close communion with Him. When the service was over, she came to me and said, "Sister Gwen, I am Christiana Willens." She went on to say that she came from Quetta, which lies to the north, in the foothills of the Himalayas.

I had heard of Miss Willens before. In fact, I had just sent a telegram to her several days earlier, telling her that we could not come, we were fully booked with meetings. Now suddenly, she was here. We invited her to our room and listened as she poured out her heart.

"Sister Gwen, ever since I heard about you some years ago, I prayed that God would send you to my city. Even when people said you were not interested in Pakistan, and would never come, I prayed for God to speak to you and call you to come to my city. When your telegram came, saying you could not come, I knew I had to come and speak to you myself. I beg you," she said with hands folded and tears in her eyes, "Come to my city. Our people need God. They need your ministry. I have come all this way, two days' and two nights' journey, and I cannot go back without you."

I turned away from the desperate, pleading look in those big brown eyes. One gets pretty accustomed to saying "No!" to invitations, but something had touched my heart, and I, too, had to weep. Oh, the need of mankind for the message of God!

"You MUST come, sister. I know it's God's will. We have prayed and prayed, and now I know God will send you to us."

"But sister," I began, "we are all booked up. We have no free time."

But faith never takes "No" for an answer. I could feel her heartbreak, and see her mountains full of lost souls. Finally I said, "Let us pray, and see what God shows us."

It is sometimes a dangerous thing to pray, because you might get a new command to do something you had not expected, and that is what happened now.

As we bowed our heads and listened, God showed us that the only thing to do was to send Sigi on alone to the next meetings. When the present meetings were over, I would fly to Quetta and join Sigi later. Thanking the Lord for showing us the answer, I told the plans to Sister Christiana. She was full of thanksgiving to God.

We made our plans, and she left to return home and prepare for my coming.

"HE IS A DEVIL"

As I boarded the plane to fly to Quetta, I noticed a little Muslim woman waiting at the bottom of the steps. She was completely covered in the customary black burka,[1] which Muslim women still wear in public. It covered her from the top of her head to the tip of her toes. It not only covered her face, but her hands were also invisible, as the long, full sleeves fell down far below her wrists. Only her small feet, shod in fine black leather shoes were visible. Travelling with her was a tall, light-skinned, bearded man, fully clothed in white, two neatly dressed little boys, and an older woman who appeared to be a nursemaid to the two children. I knew they must be a rich family, for only the business people and the well-to-do can afford to travel by air. The majority go by train and bus.

A strange thing happened as I watched her waiting for permission to climb the steps into the plane. I began to feel a great love for her fill my heart. This strange little creature, hidden beneath her robes, whose face I couldn't see — I loved with a great inflow of the love of God. I wanted to go up to her and put my arms around her. I felt her heartache and sadness. I stared at the man with her. Was he her husband, or her father? I felt he must be her husband. How old was she? What was he? He looked like a kind of "holy-man." Was he a Persian priest? I thought they must be from Iran, or somewhere in the Middle East. His eyes were cold and forbidding.

When we finally were able to board the plane, we were told we could choose any seat available. I took the closest one to her, a window seat directly in front of her.

I have seen thousands of women in Muslim dress, with veiled face, but nothing had ever gripped my heart like this before. Here was a woman I had never seen before, and even now, could not see. When the luncheon was served, I wondered how she would eat behind her veil. I hoped for a glimpse of her hands. Finally, I saw them, beautiful, young hands of a woman in her youth. Tears of love and compassion for her filled my eyes. I hastily arose, and went to the lavatory. Here, with my hands gripping the sink I cried, "Oh God, save her soul. Oh Lord, she is so precious. I don't know how to reach her, but You can." Here I prayed for her with tears, and a love that was not my own.

When I resumed my seat, one of her boys had started fussing and crying. I handed him my pen and tried to amuse him, but he would not be diverted, and he cried and fussed all the way to Quetta. His father seemed to take no notice. In these lands, children are usually the responsibility solely of the women and the servants.

The plane was flying on to Lahore, and I thought my co-passengers would surely be continuing their journey on to Lahore. I was pleased, however, to discover that when the captain announced we would soon be landing in Quetta, they were getting ready to disembark.

The welcome sight of Christiana waiting for me filled my heart with joy. Standing with her were Gustav and Helga Erickson, missionaries from Scandinavia. Helga was holding a small baby in her arms. After smiles and handshakes and welcoming kisses, Christiana suddenly exclaimed, "Oh, Sister Gwen, look who you travelled with! That man behind you. People say he is a devil. He is a very powerful person and has great influence here in these regions. People worship him as god. He does miracles. His poor little wife has a very hard time. They say she suffers much from him."

Now I knew why I had felt this burden. I broke away from my friends and went over to the man and his wife. I told them goodbye and said, "I trust your son will be all right now."

The man was surprised that I addressed him, and he answered me in flawless English, "Thank you for your concern."

As I said goodbye to his little wife, I heard her whisper to me in perfect English from behind her veil, "Thank you." My heart leaped inside of me to realize she, too, knew English.

On our way back into the city, I was further told how this man was considered a "great one," with the power of God.

People came from everywhere to visit him. He was like Simon of Acts who also had strange power to do miracles. Because of his strange power the whole district feared him. Some said, "He is a god," and others, "He is a devil." His wife was the daughter of a very high government official, and in her youth had been educated by an English God-fearing private governess, who had no doubt taught her about Jesus. Even then, there was in the city a Pakistani Christian woman who had cared for her as a child.

Upon hearing this, I begged Christiana to please go and see this woman, and ask her to try to gain an audience for me with her. She kindly visited the home and this is the story she told us.

She had a very difficult time getting permission to enter. For a long time she was kept waiting outside the house. Finally, at last she was allowed to enter and speak to the wife. When she told her about "the American woman" who had flown on the same plane with her, and who wanted to see her, and speak with her, she was told that it was impossible for her to see anyone. She was virtually kept a prisoner of this man, with no freedom to come and go. But she thanked her for my concern, and said that if I came to Pakistan another time, then an opportunity would be made for me to visit her.

I was deeply disappointed. All I could do was leave her in God's hands and pray for her. Little did I know what a great door the Lord would open for me. But that is later in the story, and a later visit to Pakistan.

"PLEASE KILL HIM.
WE CAN'T KEEP HIM."

Driving back to the city, I noticed that the wee infant carried in the arms of Helga Erickson was acting very strangely. In fact, it seemed lifeless. Its brown little nose had turned white. Mrs. Erickson was shocked to find it did not respond when she tried to awaken it. "Baby David," she called, "open your eyes."

But there was no response. Being a nurse herself, she felt for its pulse, but couldn't feel a thing. It seemed like Baby David was either dying, or had died already.

All of us became alarmed. Here I was, just having arrived, and before I even had set my feet inside the door, right in front of me, was this challenge – a tiny brown bundle of flesh and blood. "Oh Lord," I whispered, "don't let this baby die."

I reached across the seat and laid my hand gently on this seemingly lifeless form and asked Father in Heaven to let him live. Immediately there was a sign of life, and that same day I heard him crying lustily.

But then, would his parents have cared much if he had died? Certainly not, for he had had the misfortune of being born out of wedlock. His Muslim father, a prominent man, had more than one wife. This is not considered an evil thing, for all Muslims are permitted to have four wives by their law. But the trouble began when he fell in love and had an illicit relationship with a woman before he had an opportunity to marry her. Much to his consternation she had become pregnant, and then it was impossible to bring into his harem an obviously pregnant wife. The only thing remaining was to wait until the birth of the child, dispose of it secretly, and then have a proper wedding. In this way, nobody would know the difference.

But the problem was, how to do it secretly. So it was that Christiana was approached because she was a well-known and capable nurse and midwife. Fearfully and with great embarrassment, the father asked her first to try to bring about an abortion.

Sister Christiana, being a godly woman, refused to consider such a proposal. Instead, she scolded the man for his sin and told him it was wrong to cover one sin with another. "Sir, if you will repent of this, your sin, God will forgive you, but if you do an evil still greater, then God cannot forgive you." The man was a God-fearing Muslim and he was greatly shaken by her solemn warning, but he didn't know what to do with the baby.

"But sister," he pleaded, "what will I do, if my people find out? They will cut off my nose. This is a terrible sin that I have done. My life is in danger."

"Don't you worry. I will look after the baby. I will give it to good people to raise it."

The man was partially relieved. Christiana was sworn to utmost secrecy. No one dared say a thing about it or the man's whole life and social prestige would be lost.

He took the woman into his home and quietly moved away from the town into an area where no one knew him. He had to confide in his first wife, and she accepted the situation. What else could she do? She was a good woman and did not want to make trouble either. She, too, knew the wrath of her people, and how terrible it could be.

So this pregnant woman was hidden behind veiled walls to await the birth of her child. No one ever saw her.

At last the time of life came around, and Christiana was called. In the darkness of the night she helped the woman as she gave birth to a baby boy. When she turned to leave, the father thrust the baby into her arms, saying, "Take him and keep him, or kill him."

Christiana took the little brown-skinned bundle of life and brought him home. A few days later she gave him to the Ericksons to look after.

And so it was, that the little unwanted, unloved, sickly infant was carried to their house. They loved him immediately, and offered to keep him.

"But what should we call him?" they asked each other. Gustav knew that to name a child was a very important thing, and so he fasted and asked God to give him this child's name. That evening he had the answer. "He shall be called David."

Later the Ericksons had to return to their homeland on furlough and they gave him to Sister Christiana to keep. He is a beautiful boy now. His parents have married, and they have had another child. The mother was told that the baby died, and she believes it. Whenever Christiana meets the father on the street, he speaks to her, but he never asks about the child and seems to have no interest in it. To him, the child is dead. Anyway, he does not want to be reminded of his sin.

GOD'S GLORY FELL

The night of my arrival in Quetta, the meetings started in the busti. A busti is a place sectioned off in a town or a city, where the poor people live. Many of these poor people were farm labourers before the partition. After the Pakistanis took over that part of the Punjab where they lived, these people lost their jobs. They went into the cities looking for work. They had much difficulty, and because of the facts that they had little or no education and that many of them were Christians, they had to suffer. They took the only work available, that of sweeping out houses. This put them in the low-caste bracket.

The Muslims did not want these people to live amongst them, so they sectioned off areas near hospitals, and T.B. sanitoriums, and dairy farms, where there was mud which they could use to build their huts. Most of the inhabitants in these colonies are not true Christians, but the fact that many are neither Muslim or Hindu, puts them here in this category. The government says that by keeping them together in one colony, they can be better "protected."

The meetings were outside, and hundreds of men, women, and children crowded around and sat on the mat on the ground, while I mounted a shaky platform and preached to them by kerosene light.

The next morning we had a meeting indoors which I had especially called to teach these people the deeper things of God. For over an hour I spoke about the infilling of the Holy Spirit to the group which had crowded into the meeting room. I told them about my own experience, how God had given me this precious gift at the age of 17, one month after my conversion, while I was praying with my mother and a girl friend.

I told them about the glory of that wonderful hour when all my heartache and burden was lifted, and a joy beyond that of mortals filled my being. . . . "It seemed as if I would be translated. I was in the very presence of Almighty God. And as I tried to worship and praise Him, my English tongue was inadequate to express the great adoration of my soul, and suddenly, as angel wings touched me, the Holy Spirit filled my adoring soul, and the glorious celestial song of praise broke out from my innermost being, falling over my lips and tongue in an unknown language.

"On and on I sang in this new heavenly language of the Holy Spirit, and as I sang, my soul was being healed of all its past hurts, pains, and anguish. Its mistakes and failures, too, were washed away in the glorious flow of God's power. This was the closest to heaven I have ever been in my life, and it is so sacred to me, I hardly dare share it with others, lest the unbelieving and sceptical heart mock it in ridicule and thereby sin against the Holy Spirit of God.

"I remember that as I sang, I wondered at the words which I sang, and asked Father to tell me what these strange and beautiful words meant. Suddenly, the interpretation came, as the Holy Spirit continued to worship God from my heart, which now belonged to Him completely."

I finished telling this story to these hungry, humble children of God, and related how from that wonderful day on, I had a new love for God, a new consecration, and a new power to witness, which I had never before possessed.

When I asked how many desired this same experience, many raised their hand. I asked the curious and the others to quietly leave. When the group of hungry-hearted ones remained, I led them in a prayer of confession of all sin. For one's heart must be clean before His Holy Spirit can come into the body, and make it the temple of God.

The Spirit of God fell upon all who prayed. Tears began to roll down their cheeks. As we laid hands on them, one after another was gloriously filled with His Holy Spirit. And many received the beautiful gift of tongues. Truly God is no respecter of persons. This visitation was from heaven, and its results were explosive. It began a spiritual awakening in the place.

"SHE IS DYING,
COME AND PRAY FOR HER"

One morning during the service, two nurses rushed into the meeting. I saw them speaking excitedly to Christiana. She turned to me and said, "There is a woman in the mission hospital who is very sick. She has had a miscarriage, and they want you to come and pray for her."

I turned to them and asked, "Is it really that bad?"

"Yes, sister," they answered. "She is dying. Please come and pray for her."

In front of me were the people, all waiting for me to begin to minister. Could I disappoint them by leaving? And if I stayed, and the woman died, what then? Desperately I asked for guidance. Then I clearly saw how God alone is the Author and Preserver of Life, and if I did His work, which was then in my hands to do, He could hold the life of this woman in her body until I could get there.

Two hours later, when the meeting was over, we were on our way to the hospital. As we walked out on the street, we stopped a motor rickshaw. It is a three-wheeled motorized passenger vehicle, which comes to passengers, and is driven by a man in front. Every time you get into one of these suicide traps you take your life in your own hands.

On the way there, I was told the story of the one who was dying. The woman had once been a Christian, married to a man of her own religion. She had borne him two children. But his work had kept him away from home for long periods of time, and soon there grew a distance of heart and spirit between them, and she was lonely. Then one day she met a Muslim man who loved her. He wanted to make her his wife, and so, after a divorce, she married him, and in doing so, she became a Muslim officially, renouncing her Christian faith. Now she was dying of a miscarriage, and her present husband had been notified – but he was far away in another city, and couldn't get back to her in time.

Was this the judgment of God on her? Some thought it was. And, I thought, how strange that after having two husbands, that when she was dying – she had none.

At the hospital, I was brought into the darkened room, where the dying woman lay. White-clad doctors and nurses were anxiously working over her, trying to give her an intravenous injection of glucose saline. But her veins had collapsed. On the bed she was staring wide-eyed, full of fear, gasping for each breath. In the adjoining room her relatives were anxiously pacing the floor.

Curious eyes looked at me as I stood by her bed. "Oh Father," I asked, "what is this all about? Is it Your judgment on a soul who departed from You deliberately? How do I pray?"

And then I saw our Lord. He was standing on the other side of her bed, by her head, and His expression was one of love, mercy, and forgiveness.

Suddenly I could see into her heart. All the years of loneliness, her searching for love, her longing for someone to care, the rejection, the disappointment, pain, hurt and tears. And then suddenly, her whole night was turned to light and her life was lit up by the flaming passion of a new love; all the wonder, the enchantment, and the beauty of the world was hers, for she was loved! And for this glorious thing which is always a miracle in every heart, she forsook all, even her faith – or had she? Did she still, in the deep recesses of her heart, worship the Christ who stood there by her now?

His sympathy and understanding filled my heart, and I knew that the God who is big enough to die for sinners is big enough to understand His sinful children and to give them forgiveness. As I laid my hand on her forehead, and prayed a brief prayer, I KNEW everything was going to be all right. She would live. I whispered in her ear, "You will be all right, for Jesus is here," and left.

The next day when I visited her she greeted me with a cheery "Hello." She said, "Sister, Jesus came with you to Quetta, and I deeply appreciate it that you came and prayed for me, for I know if you had not come, I would be no more. Last night I called for the pastor, and made confession, and took Holy Communion. God has given me back my life."

As I looked at this beautiful woman lying there, I knew that the One who said to the woman taken in adultery, "Neither do I condemn thee," was alive in Pakistan.

THE PATHANS

Two weeks before I flew to Quetta, Sigi and I had taken our seats at the breakfast table at the Y.W.C.A. in Karachi, when we noticed a beautiful young woman seated across from us. I wondered whether she was French or Italian, or perhaps Spanish. Her skin was as fair as a European, her hair was dark and her beautiful eyes were deep blue. She was wearing the Pakistani dress, and I was very curious about her, wondering what she was doing in Pakistan.

I asked her, "Where are you from?"

"I'm Pakistani," she answered, with a twinkle of humour in her eyes.

Seeing my surprise, she added, "I'm a Pathan."

"Pathan?" I asked. "Tell me about your people. Where did you originally come from? And where do your people live?"

"We are descendants of Abraham," she answered, much to my surprise. "We belong to the ten lost tribes of Israel. Our people live in the mountains. We do not intermarry with the other Pakistanis, but until recently have only married in our own tribes. Our blood line has remained pure these many thousands of years since our ancestors came from Babylon and Assyria to live here in these mountains. We have Bible names like Abraham, Isaac, Jacob, and so forth. For several hundred years we have been Muslims. We believe in Allah, the one true God."

Immediately there was born in my heart a desire to get to know more about these beautiful people who are so different, so strange. Two weeks had passed since this meeting and now, by the strange guidance of God, I found myself up in the mountains amongst these Pathans. What was even more wonderful, the little baby David, whose life had been saved through prayer, was a Pathan by birth.

As I drove through the streets, I saw the handsome, tall, white-skinned, bearded men. They reminded me of the ancient patriarchs of the Old Testament. At times I felt like I was living amongst the Sons of Jacob. Their women do beautiful needlework, using tiny mirrors.

One morning early, I heard voices in the courtyard. After a moment, Christiana called, "Sister Gwen, come here."

I walked out of my room; there in the yard I saw Christiana talking to a Pathan tribal woman. The woman was squatting on the ground, showing her needlework. With great interest, I asked, "What does she want?"

"She has made these pieces, and she wants to sell them."

After looking at her work, I asked, "Does she know about Jesus?"

"Ask her," suggested Christiana.

So, squatting down in front of her, to put my eyes on a level with hers, I asked, "Do you know about Jesus?"

She looked at me with a blank expression, and turning to Christiana asked, "Jesus? Who is He?"

There in the brilliant sunshine, with my heart burning with love for both the Christ and the woman in front of me, who was one of the many for whom He died, I explained slowly and carefully about Jesus, the Son of God, and Saviour of the world. Patiently, she listened to me and finally answered, as she prepared to leave, "We have our prophet, Mohammed."

This little woman is typical of hundreds of thousands more who live in the mountains in a civilization two to three thousand years old. They have their prophet, Mohammed. But oh, how my heart burns that they might have Jesus the Christ!

"BRING 12 WOMEN UNTO THESE MOUNTAINS."

Daily, I used to listen to Christiana tell me stories about her medical work amongst these people. She loved them, had lived with them many years, and learned their language. Because of this, she had won their confidence.

"Sister," she used to say, "you must come again and stay longer in these mountains. I will take you to all the places. The need is very great. We must get the message of Jesus Christ to these people."

And as I listened, the burden grew. I felt so small and helpless. What could I do? By myself I was nothing. God needed many to go, not just one. And then one day He spoke to me.

"My daughter, bring 12 women into these mountains – women who all feel the burden to help these people." He showed me that the only requisites were a burden for the people, a love for them, and a willingness to lay down their lives if necessary. For the Pathans are very religious and zealous Muslims, even to the point of fanaticism. The Lord also showed me that the age of the 12 women would make no difference, neither their education nor background. Speaking to me, God said, "In this place I will speak to you, for in this place I have set up My tabernacle of prayer and My tower of praise. From here I will send out rays of glory and blessing which shall stretch out to the remotest areas of these tribal regions. Think it not strange concerning the burden which has come upon thee, for behold, I, even I the Lord, have laid this burden upon thee by My Holy Spirit. Thou has but begun to feel what I have felt for a long time. Many handmaidens of the end-time, to whom I have spoken, and whom I have prepared, shall take up this burden, and shall succeed. My end-time angel shall work with you for the salvation of the tribal people. I have prepared all things for you, and you shall be amazed at My provision and My divine provision and My divine arrangement – ordered in all things and SURE."

As I shared this burden with Christiana, she clasped her

hands in thanksgiving to God. She promised to open her home and make all preparations for our return.

As I boarded the plane to fly to Lyallpur to meet Sigi, I was happy. I knew I would come back to these mountains; but not alone, there would be 12 women with me.

THE TONGA RIDE

Sigi and our interpreter, William Evans, met me when I arrived in Lyallpur. They had been having great meetings. Thousands had attended. I was glad to hear the good news of what God had done. We climbed into a tonga (a two-wheeled cart pulled by a horse which usually is on the verge of starvation). Every time I think of Pakistan I see tongas and skinny horses, with a driver holding a whip. One time I got so upset at the driver for continually hitting his horse that I seized the whip out of his hand and held it all the rest of the way. It was only with the utmost restraint that I didn't use it on the driver himself.

An hour later we arrived at our meeting place. A great crowd had already gathered and were waiting for the meeting to start.

Standing among them was a large man with flashing black eyes and a thick, grizzly beard. He was dressed in a light-coloured priestly-looking robe. A cross hung on a chain around his neck. I wondered who he was. He was certainly different from anyone I had seen in my whole life.

At the conclusion of the service, and after having prayed for the new converts and those who needed healing, we had a late supper in someone's home. While at the table, I asked the people about this strangely dressed person. They told me that he was not known to them, since he had come only for these meetings. I determined to find out more about him.

As we were returning to the room where we would spend the night, I saw the uniquely attired man making his bed on the platform of the tent where the meetings were being held. I walked up to him and through our interpreter said, "We welcome you to these meetings, and are glad you have come."

GOD'S MYSTIC

In the past years I had read about a few mystics but I had not had the privilege of knowing any. The dictionary defines a mystic as a person who believes that God can be known directly.

This man knew God and His Son Jesus in just such a way. No mortal had introduced him to Christ, or taught him the things he knew.

Abdul was born the son of a Muslim priest. In his youth he studied in a strict Muslim school. In the curriculum was the subject of religion. They were expected to learn the Muslim faith and become experts in it. To sharpen their minds they used to hold open debates about religion. Every Thursday one student would be chosen to take the part of a Christian, one a Hindu, and one a Muslim. It happened that he always took the part of the Christian. The others would argue with him, proving from the Koran that Christianity was wrong. In order to argue better with his opponents, he studied and memorized much of the Koran. He knew pages of it by heart. Although he had never read a Bible, and knew practically nothing about the Christian faith, he became so efficient in his argument, that he was able to show the invalidity of the Muslim religion through error simply by quoting from the Koran! He won every argument, many prizes, and at the age of 12, graduated with honours, but with his faith shaken in the Muslim religion.

He told me how at times great heart-searching and doubts would grip him. In his heart the question would come, "Suppose the Muslim faith was NOT the true faith of God? Suppose Christianity WAS the true way?" After all, nobody, not even his professors could withstand his arguments. The doubts plagued him and drove him from one mosque to another, one priest to another. Always it was the same. No one could prove him to be wrong.

Persecution began. One priest became so angry that he beat him in the face, breaking out two of his front teeth. With his mouth bleeding, and holding his two teeth in his hand, he said, "Sir, beat me, and take all my teeth, but first prove to me that I am wrong."

Always, no matter where he went, they could give him no answer to satisfy him, and instead, they persecuted and beat him. As a result, he had no place to live in Pakistan. So he went to Afghanistan without a passport.

There, in Kabul, he met many religious Muslims, learned men. Again he started discussing Christianity with them. Many were Pathans. He was attacked by them and severely wounded in the head. They thought he was dead and threw him in the hills. When he came to his senses, he washed himself in a nearby fountain and went back to the men who thought they had killed him. They were so frightened at the sight of him that they turned white and began trembling and begged him to leave their area and go away.

He continued his wanderings through Afghanistan and crossed the border into Iran, again without a passport. He was then 17 years old. Sometimes he would get a ride, but most of the time he walked.

When he went to a mosque he would say to the priest, "I am a Christian, but I want to become a Muslim. Please give me the answer to some questions." Upon hearing this, they were very glad to take him in. Often he would stay with them for as many as six months. This usually ended with their getting angry with him and throwing him out.

From Iran he went to Iraq, and then to Egypt where he spent six months in the greatest Muslim University in the world and the greatest in the Middle East, the Jama Al-Azhaar. Thousands of young people attend this great university with a faculty of approximately seven hundred teachers. He spent the entire time in discussions with all these teachers. None could refute him.

From there he went to Mecca and Medina, where again he

had discussions at their great centers. From Arabia he went to Jordan, Bethlehem and Jerusalem, where he spent many months debating with the priests and religious leaders. His travels took him to Kuwait and then slowly, after three years there, back to Pakistan. He had spent 13 years in travel, all by foot, without one contact with any church or missionary or Christian of any kind.

Many times he was beaten; he carries 41 wounds in his head alone. I asked if it were hard for him to love his enemies. He said that when someone comes to him in anger, he takes off his shoe and gives it to the angry one that he might beat him. He told me that he prays for his enemies all the time.

I asked him if he had ever been in prison or jail, and he said, "Many times. This is my life."

He told me how he lives on bread and water and then he said, "I need nothing else. My Lord gives me a big, strong body." And the size of him proved that.

"Do you believe you will someday die for Jesus?" I asked.

He told me, "If I die, God will raise many more like me."

I asked, "Does God ever speak to you? Do you hear His voice?"

"So many times. God tells me often all the circumstances of a situation before they happen. Many times I have heard the voice of Jesus with my own ears. Also, I have seen angels. One time while in Quetta, someone caught my hand as I slept and pulled it. Then I heard a voice say, 'Rise up and preach for Me' — which I did."

Last of all I asked him if he thought the Muslims would soon accept Jesus Christ.

He replied, "If they are invited by sincere ones, they will accept. But the stubborn ones will refuse."

He has been rejected by his family, and sad to say, even many of the church people do not understand him. His great sorrow is that he cannot go home to his mother. "I still cannot return home openly. Only secretly at night. And now my little sister, too, believes in Jesus, but no one dares to know it. Her life would be in danger."

There were tears in our eyes when he finished telling us how Christ had led him and spoken to him. "There are many things," he said, "I cannot tell. They are too sacred to me."

"Brother," I said, "you will yet go many times to prison and perhaps even die for Christ."

He smiled and said, "This would be my greatest joy, to die for my Lord."

As we walked to the meeting after our conversation, Sigi said, "Gwen, we have seen a real man."

We had never met a man like him. We didn't even know such men of faith and courage and selflessness still existed. May God bless him wherever he is, if he is still among men.

LED BY THE SPIRIT

It is a great tragedy that many sincere children of God do not know how to be led by the Spirit. They have never learned to "hear" the voice of God. Perhaps this is because they live more in the carnal, earthly realm. For God is a Spirit, and we are told that the Father's true worshippers are those who worship Him in the Spirit. Yes, it is even for these the Father seeks and desires. While it is true that the flesh and its senses of sight, taste, and hearing can sometimes tingle with the touch of His glory, God is seldom revealed through the five human and mortal senses. But rather, He is revealed through the Spirit of man making contact with the Spirit of God.

If we rely on our natural eye to see, our natural ear to hear, and our fingers to touch, as Thomas did,[2] then we are living on the earthly plane, and God in His full glory can never be revealed to us.

One year after you are dead, your eyes, ears, and other faculties of your senses will have decayed away. Your beautiful eyes which captivate the souls of others, will be nothing but pieces of rot. Perhaps, mother, you have eyes that can pierce your children into fear and subjection. One moment after you die, they will stare out vacantly into space, like a lifeless glass eye.

Today you watch the sky with heart enthralled as the rays of the setting sun gloriously tint it in colours of gold, coral, pink and fuschia. When you have heard the last summons, and your soul has left its body, leaving it to rot and decay, you shall yet be able to see glorious scenes more splendid than the sunset which enthralled your heart as you gazed at it with natural eyes. Scenes so glorious that if you had gazed upon them with mortal eyes, you would have been smitten dead by the impact of their brilliance, for no man can see God and live. (Exodus 33:20) God was speaking our language when He used this expression with Moses. He meant that mortal flesh would consume itself in the presence of Almighty God.

Yes, even though your ear, both outer and inner, is decayed in the grave, still you will hear the music of heaven, whose glorious symphonies far surpass the creation of earth's greatest music masters. You shall eat of the fruits of heaven's orchards, and the supreme taste of honeyed sweetness shall be so delicious that one bite into heaven's fruit will make the fairest and most sumptuous earthly feasts taste like straw by comparison.

Yes, what shall you see, hear, and taste with, if these eyes, ears, and fingers are decayed in the grave, or worse still, cremated into ashes?

The faculties of touch belong to your spirit, which you even now possess, but fail to use, because no one has taught you it is possible. And so you live in the carnal and fleshly physical realm. There is little blessing in such a life, for Jesus said, "Blessed is he who has not seen (with his physical eyes) and yet believes." (John 20:29) This is indeed the blessed life; this life of the Spirit.

What are you? Are you only a body? And when the body stops functioning and rigor mortis sets in, do you cease to exist?

No, my friend! You yourself are a spirit which has been

sent to earth. Because the spirit is invisible to mortal eyes, God has given it a body to possess, in order to make contact with, and commune with other mortals. That is why God Himself became flesh and took upon Himself the body of our Adamic race, so that man could see and handle God, and live.

When you were excommunicant from your body, you were in spirit form, and as such could communicate with other spirits. So the real "you" is a spirit.

A dwelling place is only a house, until persons move into it, and then it becomes a home as it takes on the personality of the occupants. So your body with its physical features soon begins to radiate your true personality, your true spirit. A proud spirit walks proudly and makes the body put on the appearance of pride. A selfish spirit makes the hands reach out to seize for its own what it desires. A self-pitying spirit causes the mouth of its owner to murmur and complain, weeping for attention. And a happy spirit causes its owner to speak with joy and give cheer wherever it goes.

I believe as we learn to live in the spirit realm, we will be able to worship God and communicate with Him more perfectly.

In order to "hear" God, the spirit must be very still and the heart of the spirit very open and yielded to the will of God, for God's Spirit speaks very gently to us. Remember, His is still the same small voice (or gentle whisper, as it is written in the Living Word) that changed kingdoms in Elijah's day. (I Kings 19:12-18) Our trouble comes when men and religious leaders think they have heard God in the storm, the earthquake, and the fire. And so they have "come down from the mount of God" with a message of judgment and terror. Had they waited longer, until they heard the gentle whisper, their message would have been changed into the gentleness of the gentle Jesus, so that they would become not only qualified to anoint men to be kings and prophets (a work only God can do), but also to be translated into the chariots of glory, as Elijah was.

There will be no translation of the saints until the spirit of man is completely reunited with the Spirit of his Creator, and then the natural will melt away and "die" in the presence of this God-indwelt-being. And the gravitations of this earth will lose its power to hold the Sons of God captive.

To be led by the Spirit is the beginning of this glorious life. Enoch walked with God, and God took him, or, as the Living Word translation says, "When he was 365-years-old and in constant touch with God, he disappeared, for God took him." (Gen. 5:24) In this life of constant communion with God, there is divine guidance. We must learn to live like this, for only in this way can we be worthy to escape the dreadful things which shall shortly come to pass on this planet. "Keep a constant watch; and pray that if possible you may arrive in My presence without having to experience these horrors." (Luke 21:36)

Most of the time I feel my life has been guided by God. I always pray that I may know His will, and have the courage to do it.

When I arrived in Lyallpur, the people begged me to stay longer, while Sigi went on alone to the next place. It seemed a wise thing to do. Here was a great crowd. The meetings were getting better all the time. There was no reason I could not stay longer. Almost, I decided to stay, but God spoke to me as I sought Him, and said, "Leave with Sigi."

The next day we read in the papers how rioting suddenly broke out in this city. Mad frenzied mobs raced through the streets, killing people, burning the post office and other buildings. Curfew was ordered. It would have been impossible to have had meetings, and I would not have been able to leave the city. How good to know our Lord had spared us these troubles, as He promised to spare those who would walk in the Spirit.

ESTHER

Sahiwal, the city where we had our next meetings, is a place which God will never forget. It is here that one of His end-time handmaidens gave her life for the Lord Jesus, her only Lover.

We stayed with two elderly women who have lived a godly life, and I still remember the beautiful times in prayer we had together. One of these dear sisters told me how she heard the voice of God speaking many times to her audibly. She told me how, that on March 19, 1969, she was awakened in the middle of the night. A tender voice, the voice of our Lord, was speaking to her in Urdu, and said these very soul-shaking words, "One week is left to preach the Gospel to the non-Christians." We all know that in Bible language, one week is seven years.

She told us how in the hours between 3:00 and 4:00 a.m. she heard the voice of God speak three times, "JESUS IS COMING IN NO TIME AT ALL."

The other of these two sisters is a nurse in the missionary hospital. It was she who told us the sad, tragic story of beautiful Esther.

Esther was born and raised a Muslim in a well-to-do family. She was sent to a mission school for her education. While there, she heard the wonderful story of Jesus. Her tender heart was opened to Him. After she returned to her home she longed to hear and read more about Him whom she had learned to love, but there was no one to tell her. She dared not share her longing with anyone. For it was a dreadful and forbidden thing to believe in Jesus.

But God saw her longing heart, and in His grace, He sent one of the missionaries to look for her. The missionary lady searched all over the city, making inquiries everywhere, until she found her.

You can imagine Esther's surprise when one day the missionary called at her home. Knowing the Muslim hatred of the Christian faith, the sister wisely refrained from mentioning anything about it. Instead, she said she was concerned about Esther's education, and hoped she would be able to continue her studies. Because the family refused to let Esther return to the school, the missionary offered to come and give her private tutoring. This was accepted by the family. When her mother left the room and ordered the servant to bring in tea, Esther whispered, "Please bring me a Bible. I want to read about Jesus." The missionary gladly promised.

The next day the missionary sister returned with an arm full of books. Hidden among them was a small New Testament. The English lessons began under the watchful eyes of the family. Neither dared speak a word about Jesus.

Finally the time to leave had come. Unobtrusively, she slipped the New Testament inside some papers, and in front of all, she handed it to Esther saying, "Study these well, and you will be a wise girl."

As soon as Esther could, she hurried into a secret place with her precious book, and began to read. When she heard footsteps, she quickly hid it, dropping it behind the bed. Hour after hour, she read eagerly the story of Jesus. Tears flowed down her cheeks, tears of joy, as she read about His love, gentleness and wisdom. Then as she travelled with Him the Calvary road, and stood in vision watching cruel hands nail Him to the cross, the tears turned to those of sorrow for her Lord. And oh, how her heart leapt with excitement, when with Mary, she found His tomb empty! And, oh, the great relief at last as He stood amongst His disciples, alive forevermore! He was, indeed, the Son of God, as the centurian soldier had proclaimed when he watched Jesus die; and He would have her heart forever, no matter what the cost! She would be His believer and follow Him even to death. Little did she realize when she made this noble resolution, that this was just the price she would have to pay.

As Esther grew to womanhood, the family decided it was time for her to marry. A young Muslim was chosen from among their acquaintances. This was a new problem for Esther. She didn't want a husband; she was already "in love" with her Saviour. She begged her family to wait, but they would not hear of it, and so she decided to do what no normal Muslim girl ever would think of doing. She ran away!

In our western civilization this is no great wonder, but in

her country and society it was a shattering thing to do. She ran straight to her missionaries and begged them to protect her and hide her.

Out of love for her, knowing how it would endanger them all, they took her into their girl's school and hid her among hundreds of other young girls.

Meanwhile, the family began to search for her. Half in anger and half in anxiety, they combed the city looking for their sister and daughter. At last they found her. But she bravely refused to return home. Finally they said she may yet stay awhile and study.

Esther was happy. She began to work for the Lord. It was at this time that she chose the name of Esther, after the beautiful woman of courage in the Bible.

With one of the missionary sisters, she travelled for months into the villages, visiting her Muslim sisters in purdah (seclusion of women from public observation; hidden away), and telling them of the One who was greater than a prophet, who was the Son of God. Her beautiful voice was lifted in praises to God constantly. Few could sing like her.

Then one day, her happiness was interrupted, when she received a letter from home demanding her to return for a marriage her family had arranged for her. Now her song was stilled, as she sought God and prayed for guidance. "We love you," the letter had said. "You are our daughter. Now it is your duty to return home and be married."

Esther longed for her people. She loved them dearly. If she said "No," she would be cut off forever from her family. Finally after days of prayer, she had reached her decision.

She wrote a letter to her family telling them she loved them and wanted to return. She even said she would be willing to get married, but he must be someone whom she could herself choose. She wanted only a Christian. The letter was prayed over, sealed, and sent by registered post. In anticipation, she packed her trunk and awaited their reply.

A week passed, and there was no letter. Another week came and went. By the third week apprehension filled her heart. The silence was uncanny, and not a good sign. She waited through the third week. During the fourth week, she became ill with a severe cold.

One evening she was suffering so badly, the missionary told her to retire early. She said goodnight and went to her room.

When she did not come out of her room the next morning, the missionary became worried, and thought she had better see if she was all right.

When she opened the door, she saw blood. Blood was everywhere . . . on the walls, on the floor, and the bed. She ran in horror up to the bed, and looking down, saw beautiful Esther's head had been chopped open by an axe-like instrument. Esther was dead!

Who had done it? The police were called in. Intensive investigations began. For days the Criminal Investigation Department searched the house, and Esther's belongings for clues. Someone said, "A jealous lover did it."

So they searched her books and papers for love letters and other evidences. After many days the head investigator confessed, "The only lover Esther had was Jesus Christ," and so the case was closed.

But, in the law courts of heaven, angels witnessed the dreadful deed, and on the day of judgment, when the books of man's deeds are going to be opened, the name and names of those who planned and executed this cruel and cold-blooded murder shall be called out to stand before God, the Judge, for judgment.

If you, who did this deed, should read these words, I call on you to repent of your sins, and ask God to forgive you. His Son Jesus, as He hung on the cross, prayed, "Father, forgive them, for they know not what they are doing." I know Esther would forgive you, for you were the ones she loved, and surely, if your repentance is sincere, God shall also forgive you, and you may spend eternity with your own beloved Esther, and her Lord Jesus, the Christ.

IS JESUS THE SON OF GOD?

The sister, who told us the story, was on duty in the hospital when Esther's dead body was brought in. She personally told us about the deep wounds in Esther's head.

The Muslims believe that Jesus is a great prophet, but when we try to tell them that He is the Son of God, they become angry. Very few dare to preach these truths openly for fear of reprisal.

When I heard this, and knew that this city was very strongly Muslim, I determined to take my stand for truth openly that night in the meeting. We had been having good attendance, and God had been blessing. Daily, souls were coming to Christ, and some were filled with the Holy Spirit. Others had been healed. The message went out over the loudspeakers, so that hundreds could listen on the outside in secret as well.

That night, as I stood to give the message of God to these people, I looked down over my audience. There were Muslim women, clothed in their black burka, sitting on the mats laid out for them on the ground. Men were there also. Crowds stood around the tent. With a clear voice I announced my text, "Is Jesus the Son of God?" For over one-and-a-half hours, I poured out my heart to this vast audience. I proved to them by the witnesses of Jesus' lifetime that He is the Son of God.

"NO TROUSERS . . . CAN'T PREACH"

It was here, also, that a humorous thing happened one morning. Sigi and I had done our washing and our clothes were still not dry when it was time for us to leave for the morning Bible study in the tent.

"What shall I do, Gwen? My trousers are not dry. Maybe I had better not go today," said Sigi.

Not realizing the true situation myself, I said, "Oh, I don't think it really matters that much. Just put on your black skirt. It is good and long, and I am sure that nobody will say anything to you about it."

So Sigi put on her white blouse and black skirt and we went to the meeting. As we were walking in the door of the tent, one of the ministers slipped up to me and said, "Sister Gwen, where are Sigi's trousers?"

"At home on the line," I answered. "We had to wash them, and they were not dry, so she came in her European clothes."

"No, no, sister, that will never do," he said, shaking his head. "She will offend the people. They are not used to seeing women without trousers. Please kindly ask her to sit at the back in the corner, where she will not be seen. She must never come on the platform without trousers."

I smiled to myself, thinking about our "holiness" preachers who, back in our own country, condemn a woman to the lake of fire for wearing trousers. If they would bring their wives to one of our great revival meetings in this part of the world, she would have to put on trousers also, or sit in the back corner in shame.

Sigi said, "I almost felt like a sinner, Gwen, because I wasn't wearing trousers."

MY BIBLE

Shanti Nagar! The name of this remote village had been on my heart for a long time. I had asked that it be included in our itinerary. Had I known how inaccessible it was, and how closed the hearts of many of the people would be there, we certainly would have had qualms about going. But God often pulls a veil over what awaits us, and like children, we rush in where angels fear to tread.

We got on a "bus," a rickety, Pakistani vehicle, consisting of a Pakistan-constructed coach and an imported motor, and travelled six hours along a hot, dusty road. When we came as far as the bus could take us, we got out. Our limbs were shaking from the "endurance test" of being shaken and bumped on small, hard, straight-back wooden seats for so long a time. The bus, as all buses in Pakistan, was loaded to the hilt. There is ALWAYS room for one more!

When we reached the end of our bus trip, we engaged a tonga, and after piling ourselves and all our luggage inside, we started along a desert-like, sandy road to Shanti Nagar. At times we had to get out and walk, while the horse pulled the tonga across difficult areas. At last, we rolled into "town." It was dark by this time, and the people were waiting anxiously, for the meeting was scheduled to begin, and we still hadn't arrived.

We were tired and dirty, and I was sad because water had accidently spilled on my good Bible and damaged it badly. My beautiful Bible which had travelled over a million miles with me and from which I had preached thousands of sermons. It was marked and underscored from beginning to end. Its pages were spotted with my tears. Only God and I know how many times I had heard Him speak to me through its pages. It had been a rod of reproof when I needed it, and often I had bowed my head in shame, as I heard His stern rebuke. But more often it had comforted me and challenged me to complete my task on earth. Once before, its covers had been worn off, and no wonder, for it had received a hard beating as I often had pounded its pages with my fists, while expounding something which had moved me with deep emotion. But the cover had been bound back on by a friend in India, and I had hoped to use it for many years.

Now I mourned its "injury" like that of a dear friend.

WOMEN ONLY!

Right from the first night, we noticed a hardness and indifference in our audience. We called for fasting the next day, hoping it would break the opposition, but the next night it was the same.

Day after day we prayed and called on God through the day and preached our hearts out at night, but it was the same. My time was limited, as I had to go to Karachi in time to fly to London for a speaking engagement I had there. I knew Sunday would be my last day in this place.

Sunday morning came; we again addressed our audience in a great outdoor meeting. There were hundreds out to every meeting, but not a single heart seemed to have been touched by God. We were a novelty and a curiosity to them. The women sat and looked at us, but didn't hear a word we said. Most of the time, some of them were talking and laughing amongst themselves or playing with their babies. The men and women were seated in separate sections, as is the custom in these countries. I could understand why Paul had told the women to keep silence in the church.[3] He must have preached in Shanti Nagar!

On the other side, their husbands watched with a critical attitude. The whole thing broke our hearts, for what to us was a serious matter of life and death (because it concerns eternal things) appeared to be no more than an interesting drama to them. I was reminded of Ezekiel 33:30-33: "Son of man, the children of thy people still are talking against thee by the walls (in their houses) and whisper about you at the doors, saying, Come on, let's have some fun! Let's go hear him tell us what the Lord is saying. So they come as though they are sincere, and sit before you listening. But they have no intention of doing what I tell them to; they talk very sweetly about loving the Lord, but with their hearts they are loving their money. You are very entertaining to them, like someone who sings lovely songs with a beautiful voice or plays well on an instrument." (I was playing my accordian in all these meetings.) "They hear what you say but don't pay any attention to it! But when all these terrible things happen to them, as they will, then they will know a prophet has been among them."

"Oh, God," I cried, "give me the key. There must be some way to reach these people. Please help us to help them know You and love You."

Suddenly I had the key! "This afternoon at five o'clock there will be a special meeting for the women," I announced.

"No man is permitted to come to the meeting. Only the women will be permitted."

The men were shocked. The women were pleased. Never had anything like this happened before.

"The first bell will ring at 4:40," I said. "When you hear it, you will know it is time to get ready. The second will ring 15 minutes later, announcing it is time to come. At five o'clock SHARP the meeting will begin. If any men come, you will be asked to leave."

It was like dropping a bomb.

At five o'clock a large group of women had gathered. We were surprised to see such a response. Even our interpreter was a woman. Christiana had joined us and was looking after us like a sharp-eyed mother hen, and so she would interpret for us while our usual interpreter, William Evans, sat this one out.

And so the "Women Only" meeting began. In the background, a few of the men shyly gathered, but they didn't dare join us. We knew they were listening, but that didn't matter, for I really had nothing to say to the women which the men couldn't hear.

Why then had I called this special separate meeting? Because I had to get the women alone. All their lives they had taken second place. As children, they were not as important as their brother. He was the one preferred and honoured. Brother had the best food, the best clothes, and the best education, even the best love of the parents. He could do anything and get away with it. He was never scolded nor spanked. His naughtiness was considered cute and a sign of intelligence, but if she tried the same thing, she was punished and told that girls don't act like that. She had no choice.

As a young woman, she had dreams of love and marriage, but again, she had no choice. Her parents did the choosing. After all, weren't they wiser than she, and, after all, what did she know about these things? So a man was chosen for her, and more likely than not, she hadn't seen him till the day of her wedding. Perhaps she was lucky, and if she were, he was a kind man. Then her life would be easier. But love? How could it be? When he didn't know her, had never seen her before. After all, she was only a body, with a name.

Sometimes they were fortunate, when through the years love grew between them and a strange and comfortable feeling of needing each other for companionship, for sex, and for what the one could do for the other, existed. But she was never his equal. He could not confide in her; after all, she was only a woman, and raising children was solely her responsibility, be there one or nine.

She had the burden of carrying them inside her womb, and then later, outside her body. She not only bore them, she nursed them at her breast, openly and unashamedly, proud of her large milk supply. Sometimes, she used to say, "I had enough for two."

And she, too, it was, who later fed them with her hands, carefully mixing the rice together with daal (a soupy mixture resembling lentil soup) and squashing it with her fingers, and then rolling it into a small ball between the thumb and two forefingers of her right hand so it would be small enough to pop into their mouths, until they themselves knew how to do it.

Washing clothes was an ordeal. If they were poor, she had no laundry soap, but there always was a stone somewhere. And so the wet garment was rolled and beat on the stone until it went to pieces more with the washing of it, than the wearing.

Ironing was never necessary. No one had an iron in the village. Clothes were laid on the ground to dry. Sometimes someone had a clothes line, a little one, but then, she didn't need a long one, for there was never that much to wash, simply because there was not that much to wear, and clothes must therefore be washed every day.

Her life was a busy one. She arose early in the morning to build her fire out of cow-dung cakes for cooking her chapatis, a flat pancake-shaped bread made out of wheat flour, kneaded and baked on a flat pan on the top of her open fire.

They need constant attention, and take much time; and sometimes, I think that half of the life of an Indian housewife is spent squatting on the ground in front of her smoking open fire, making chapatis. And, of course, she always does ALL of her cooking down on the floor, if she has a floor. Usually it's only hard pressed mud.

I have been in hundreds of Indian and Pakistani homes, and almost all are the same in the kitchen. I often wish I could give every woman in India a counter to do her cooking on, but they probably wouldn't even appreciate it. After all, this has been their custom for thousands of years. Their mothers cooked like that, their grandmothers, and their great-grandmothers, and who knows, after all, maybe even our common mother, Eve, did too!

Now, here they were in front of me, and I started telling them how important they were to God. How much He loved them. How He loved them enough to send His one precious Son to die for their sins, and how this Son wanted to be with them and help them if they would accept Him. How He promised to give them the Holy Spirit, and it was also for them . . . this great Gift, because other women long ago, even the mother of Jesus Himself, had received this Gift on the day the Spirit was outpoured.

I spoke for about 40 minutes, and even while I was speaking the tears began to fill their eyes, and run over, down their cheeks. And then I knew I had said enough, and leaving my place, I went amongst them, laying my hands on them and praying for them. The Holy Spirit fell upon these precious ones, they repented of their sins as they saw their hearts in a new way. Then their tears turned to tears of joy as God comforted them with the beautiful sweet inner conviction of forgiveness.

> *Oh, the joy of sins forgiven,*
> *Oh, the peace the blood-washed know.*
> *There is perfect peace and rest*
> *Where the healing waters flow.*

And the healing waters were flowing through Shanti Nagar that day, right from the throne of God, into these hungry hearts. They forgot themselves, they forgot their children, they forgot each other as they remembered God.

The men heard the noise and gathered around to behold this strange wonder. By that time it was time for the evening meeting, and so we invited them inside and proceeded with the next service.

And now God was there! Oh, how we preached that night! What power! What anointing! What liberty! What attention they gave! What mighty conviction!

For one-and-one-half hours I preached, and when the altar call was given for them to come forward to meet God, many came and knelt at the front, weeping with mighty conviction.

I saw one little boy about 12 years of age crying bitterly. Turning to my interpreter, I asked, "Why is he crying like that? What is he praying about?"

Tears came to his eyes. "He is saying, 'Oh God, how cruelly we have treated You, after the great love You had for us, and after suffering so greatly for us!' " And then he began to weep and pray for Pakistan as if he could see by the Spirit, even then, what great and terrible tragedy and evil was being prepared for her.

Suddenly a man stood up, pointed upwards, and cried out, "I see Jesus. He is hanging there on the cross, and He is weeping for Shanti Nagar."

People were struck with awe and fear. Many repented of their sins. God had indeed come to Shanti Nagar.

THE VISION OF THE MASSACRE

As God was blessing the people and pouring out His Spirit upon them, He called Sigi to go aside alone, and pray. He had a message for her.

There, alone in her room, as she knelt to pray, she suddenly had a vision, a terrible vision. She saw the West Pakistani soldiers open fire upon multitudes of helpless men, women, young people and children. She saw people falling, wounded and bleeding, on the streets. She knew that God was telling her that this was what was happening in East Pakistan.

The Lord said to her, "You must go to East Pakistan. There you will taste of the sufferings of the Christians."

When Sigi shared with me her vision, God confirmed to my heart that this was indeed His will. At the same time, I, too, saw the vision of ruthless mass murders of thousands of helpless and innocent people. I also was shown that Sigi would be used by God to witness to, and encourage some important person in government service. I told her about this, and later it was fulfilled.

THE TONGA DRIVER

It was still pitch dark at four in the morning when we arose after a few hours sleep and prepared to leave Shanti Nagar for Karachi. First of all there was one hour of travel by horse and tonga to get to the bus, which drove us for two hours to the city where we got the plane to fly to Karachi.

Feeling tired and half asleep, we gathered ourselves and our things together in the darkness. There was no electricity and our flashlights were dim. When we were ready, we waited for our tonga. Finally, when it got there, we were relieved — we had a long trip before we got to our plane and we had to be on time.

Unfortunately, when we went to load our things on the tonga, we found it was already loaded with grass and hay. Try as we might, there was no way to leave the straw in the tonga and get our luggage on as well.

I finally became exasperated and said, "Sir, take out your straw so we can have room for our things."

"But memsahib,"[4] he said, "my horse needs the hay. If I don't give it food it will have no strength to pull you."

We tried to argue with him that he could get food at the other end for his horse, but he wouldn't listen.

Meanwhile, it was getting late and I was becoming anxious. There were no other tongas that we could call that early in the morning. If we delayed much longer, we would miss the plane. But how could we go without our suitcases?

At last I thought of an idea.

"Sir, roll up your straw in a bundle and leave it here. We will give you extra money to buy food for your horse."

This was a fine idea — both for him and his horse! Not only would his horse still have his straw when they got back, but he would have extra money. So we got the baggage and ourselves in the tonga and started out.

I was feeling happier as I saw the morning dawn, and I began to sing. Suddenly I turned to the driver and asked, "Are you a Christian?"

"Alas!" he answered, "I cannot be one because I am a tonga driver."

"But what difference does that make?" I asked, surprised.

"Because Christians aren't supposed to tell lies, and if I told no lies, I'd soon be broke and be a poor man. In this business one must not only be a liar, but a good one, and one must know how to cheat also."

I didn't know for a moment whether to laugh or cry. He was so serious.

"Would you not like to be a Christian, and have peace in your heart?" I asked.

"Oh yes, memsahib. That I would. I get so tired of my life, and my sinful doings. But what is there to do? I have a wife and family."

"Did your wife come to our meetings?"

"Oh yes, she came and her life was changed. Now she is a Christian. She wept and confessed her sin and has peace. Oh, it would indeed be nice to be a Christian, but it's no use considering it, as long as I am a tonga driver."

"Sir," I answered, "if you will be an honest man, and take Jesus as your Saviour, and partner, He will ride with you on this tonga and His blessing will be with you and you will be not only a happy man, but prosperous, too."

"Then I would like to be a Christian."

"Would you like to pray now?" I asked.

"No, when we get there. I must first do my job. I must get you there."

"But there will be a lot of people who will see you pray. Don't you think it will be better to pray here alone with us?"

"About people, I don't care, even if the whole world sees me. Now I've made up my mind to be a Christian, the sooner they see me pray, the better." He was silent for a while and then he added, "And the more that see me, the better, too."

I wondered if he were looking for an excuse, but when we arrived at the town and prepared to board the loaded bus, he turned to me and said, "Now, you may pray for me."

And right there in front of all the people, while the bus waited, he gave his heart to Jesus Christ. God bless the tonga driver wherever he is today; God bless his wife and family; and oh yes, Lord, his horse, too!

When we got back to Karachi we found that there was a national alert. The country was in a state of war. The full facts of what was going on were completely covered up by the authorities. Even the mail was censored.

Sigi was preparing to leave for East Pakistan by air, and I was preparing to go to London. The night before I left, as we prayed with a great burden for both East and West Pakistan, God gave someone a vision that showed us that out of the rubble and ruin of this warfare would come a great harvest of souls.

I hated to leave Sigi by herself. I knew she had a hard commission. But I knew it was God's will and I dared not interfere. As I boarded the plane to fly away, I picked up the latest newspaper in the aircraft. And there was the true story told on the front page: The story of the mass murder of innocent people in East Pakistan by the West Pakistan troops, the story of the pillage and rape and cruelty of war, of the burning of villages and ransacking of houses, of a country in turmoil and the throes of rebirth.

I looked out of the window, and saw Sigi standing there,

bravely waving me goodbye. "Oh, if only I could tell her the true story! If only I could warn her! None of this was known by the ordinary people in West Pakistan.

I knew now what very great danger she would have to go through. I felt like getting off the plane. I wondered if there was any way I could warn her, but we were separated and even though she was only a few yards away, it was as if I were already in another country.

As the plane taxied down the runway, my heart ached for her, that slip of a girl, standing there, bravely holding back her tears.

Only God alone knew what would happen before we would meet again.

Part Two

Many westerners still wonder what the Bangladesh war was all about. Sad to say, we have become so self-centered, that while a world is in turmoil, and lies on the brink of destruction, we shrug our shoulders like our ancestor who murdered his brother, and ask the question, "Am I my brother's keeper?"[5]

For those who are interested, I will try to explain the background that led to civil war in Pakistan.

During the time of the British occupation of India, India and Pakistan were one. There was no Pakistan then. But there was continual unrest in India between the Muslims and the Hindus, the two great religions of the people. After many years of dispute which often erupted into terrible bloodshed and killings between Muslims and Hindus, the British yielded to the desire of the Muslims to give them their own land. Just before the British left India, they sliced off a portion on the northeast and another on the northwest. This was Pakistan.

And so Pakistan became an independent nation in August 1947, after its partition from India. The reason for its desire for separation from India was understandable, for there were millions of Muslims who had lived under the dominance of a Hindu India, and they wanted their own ideological Islamic nation.

But religion makes a poor binding when it is not cemented by persecution, and when persecution from the Hindus stopped, they found they had very little in common.

Not only was Pakistan separated by 1,200 miles of Indian territory, but her peoples were completely different in race and culture.

In West Pakistan lived the big, tall, hardy frontiersmen — men who had struggled centuries for survival from a dry, barren land of mountains and sand.

The Bengalis in the east are a world apart — gentle dreamers, musicians, and poets who have become accustomed to an easy abundance from their delta homeland. Rainfall is plentiful. As a result there are two major rice crops a year. Eighty percent of the world's production of raw jute comes from the east. In addition, they have sugarcane, tea and grain.

Situated on the Bay of Bengal, and having numerous rivers and streams, East Pakistan is a major fish-producing area. Besides this, there have been 11,100 industrial establishments. Of these, the more important ones were 22 textile mills, 7 sugar factories, 18 match factories, 7 glass works, 178 hosiery factories, 29 jute mills, and 28 aluminum works. Production of paper in 1966-1967 was 26,500 tons and newsprint, 35,400 tons.

For those interested in wildlife, East Pakistan possesses a great abundance of wildlife, including big game such as Bengali tigers, crocodiles, elephants, leopards, and various species of large cats.

Yet, in spite of all this wealth, the people have remained poor. A per capita income of 98 rupees compares poorly with 178 rupees in West Pakistan: the reason being that since 1947, East Pakistan had been subjected to economical exploitation by the military rulers of West Pakistan. The Bengalis claimed that throughout the 25 years, West Pakistan made use of the external trade of East Pakistan to further their own interests. There was a famous, though exaggerated, statement made in East Pakistan: "The streets of Karachi were paved in gold, while our own people starve."

West Pakistan took the larger share of development projects and foreign aid. The badly needed foreign exchange was used to develop Karachi and the Punjab. The most tragic part of it was that the wealth of East Pakistan was drained away to West Pakistan, not for the benefit of the people of West Pakistan, but for the enriching of 22 wealthy families. These families shared about 90 percent of the wealth of the country.

As late as November 8, 1971, President Yahya Khan confessed, "No one ever treated the Bengalis fairly. East Pakistan was down and out, and we did not pay sufficient attention to its development."

As to foreign development aid, only 20 percent foreign exchange earnings of East Pakistan were Rs. 1,125 crores,[6] in contrast to West Pakistan 815 crores, but East Pakistan was allowed to spend only Rs. 540 crores, in contrast to West Pakistan which spent Rs. 1,400 crores.

It has also been pointed out that people of East Pakistan were denied opportunities of training under international arrangements. Only 100 East Pakistanis, as opposed to 732 West Pakistanis, were trained under the United Nations scheme. The same was true under the Columbia plan, 150 East Pakistanis were trained and 1,431 West Pakistanis.

It was stated that in West Pakistan the government spent Rs. 3,000 crores, as against Rs. 500 crores in East Pakistan on non-development expenditures by the central government. All this occurred in spite of the fact that the population of East Pakistan was 75 million, in West Pakistan, 38 million.

Quaid i-Azam Mohammed Ali Jinnah, the much-loved, founding-father of Pakistan, told the people, "Forget you are Muslims, Hindus, Christians and Parsis; think of yourselves only as Pakistanis."

Not all Muslims had left India to come to Pakistan; 40 million stayed behind. Neither did all the Hindus leave the part of India which became Pakistan. Pakistan inherited more than 15 million Hindus, mostly in East Pakistan.

But Jinnah did not survive very long, and others who followed him cast his words of wisdom aside, and so the two wings drifted apart.

In 1950, the East Pakistan leaders raised their voices against the injustice. They desired that the Bengali language, which was the language they spoke, should be declared the official language of East Pakistan.

In 1954, the original Muslim League Assembly Party was completely routed in the provincial election and was replaced by the United Front of East Pakistan of the Awami League and the Krishah Shramih Party — both of whom came into power and formed the government. The West Pakistan rulers refused to accept the victory of the people of East Pakistan and proclaimed governors-rule, after dismissing the ministry and the assembly. This was a great setback to democracy in East and West Pakistan.

In 1958, came the Martial Law Regime which was looked upon as a powerful attempt of the military to perpetuate West Pakistan's political and economic dominion over the majority of people living in East Pakistan.

In 1961, President Ayub tried to bring a compromise by offering a few changes which were unacceptable to the people of East Pakistan, and the gulf widened even more.

The people of East Pakistan wanted, political and economic rights and felt no sacrifice too great for their achievement. They rose as one man against the dictatorship — Ayub resorted to ruthless, brutal force to crush the democratic movement of East Pakistan. A reign of terror began. All popular leaders were arrested; resentment and anger spread. Widespread unrest shook the country. The army was called out to maintain law and order; the people refused to yield to fear and continued their struggle. There were major strikes with thousands arrested. Many were killed by police bullets. The people demanded Ayub release Sheikh Mujibur Rehman, a political prisoner. Upon his release, he led the people and demanded on their behalf full regional autonomy for both East and West Pakistan, but was refused.

On March 25, 1969, Ayub could not face the onslaught of the angry people. He passed on the ruling power to General Mohammed Yahya Khan who imposed martial law and dissolved national and provincial assemblies. He promised general elections in December, 1970.

On December 7, 1970, just about three months before Sigi and I arrived in Karachi, there were general elections in all of Pakistan. In East Pakistan the Awami Party, headed by Sheikh Mujibur Rehman, secured an overwhelming majority. In West Pakistan, the Pakistan People's Party, headed by Z.A.

Bhutto, secured the majority. On the basis of the total number of seats in the National Assembly, Mujibur Rehman was entitled to become the Prime Minister of Pakistan and to take the leading part in drafting the constitution for Pakistan. He demanded that the constitution be based on his party's six points.

The six points were:

1. That a federal form of government be established.

2. That the Federal government control only defense and foreign policy.

3. That two separate currencies for East and West Pakistan be introduced, or if a single currency were to be maintained, there would be a stoppage of flow of wealth into West Pakistan.

4. That the States would have exclusive authority to levy taxes; federal expenses to be met by a uniform percentage of all state taxes.

5. That separate external trade accounts be maintained by each state.

6. That a militia force, an ordinance factory, a military academy, and naval headquarters be set up in East Pakistan.

On December 28, Mr. Bhutto voiced disagreement with Mr. Rehman's call for provincial autonomy.

In February of 1971, Gen. Yahya Khan fixed March 3 for National Assembly Session. Two days later, Mr. Bhutto threatened to boycott the Assembly sessions if Mr. Rehman did not accommodate the views of his party in constitution-making. He also announced that none of the 85 Assembly members of his party would dare to attend the session called by Khan for March 3 for if anyone dared to go he "would break his bones." He also sought to postpone the inauguration of the National Assembly to facilitate talks between the leaders of the Awami League and the People's Party (Rehman and himself).

On March 1, Gen. Khan postponed the Assembly Session and fired East Pakistan's Governor, Vice-Admiral S.M. Ahsan.

Mr. Rehman called for a general strike in Dacca to protest

against the postponement of Assembly Sessions. Resentment erupted into violence in Dacca, and troops moved into action. Curfew was imposed.

On March 3, the Awami League launched a "non-cooperative" movement. Rehman rejected Gen. Yahya Khan's invitation to a conference of political leaders.

On March 5, 300 persons were killed in East Pakistan army action against the Awami League volunteers and the people.

Mujibur Rehman asked government servants to take orders from him. He asked the people not to pay taxes and declared that his party would attend the Assembly Inauguration set by Gen. Khan for March 25 only if martial law was lifted.

The civil disobedience movement was launched and East Pakistani judges refused to swear in Lt. General Tikka Khan as the new Governor. (He later was named the "butcher of Bengal.")

On March 7, Sheik Mujibur Rehman spoke at the Ramma Race Course in Dacca, East Pakistan, before tens of thousands of people.

On March 14, the central government issued an ultimatum asking workers to return to work by March 15.

On March 15, Rehman announced a unilateral declaration of autonomy. Gen. Yahya Khan arrived in Dacca for talks.

On March 19, he and Rehman began constitutional talks.

On March 21, Bhutto arrived and conferred with Yahya Khan.

On March 25, constitutional talks were deadlocked, and more killings were reported. The army took vantage position and started shooting demonstrators on a massive scale. Mujibur Rehman declared East Pakistan a sovereign independent People's Republic of Bangladesh and civil war broke out in different parts of the country with West Pakistani troops arriving in large numbers. That same night Yahya and Bhutto secretly flew back to West Pakistan, much to the surprise of Rehman. They declared Rehman to be a rebel, charging him with treason.

As American-supplied tanks rolled into Dacca on the night

of March 25, a column of troops sped to Dacca University. Every student in the hostel was killed. One student walking from a nearby hotel screamed, "My God, my God, they are killing them all!" Simultaneously, the greatest exodus in history began. From Dacca alone, 10,000 persons left within a couple of hours. This would continue for nine months, until ten million refugees would flee into India from all over East Pakistan (Bangladesh). During the first two days, more than 150,000 people were killed in Bangladesh. Heaps of corpses were lying all along the road leading to the university. Aircraft, tanks and artillery were used on the helpless people who were armed with little more than courage.

On March 26, Mujibur Rehman was arrested and flown to a secret place in West Pakistan where he was imprisoned.

On March 28, a Provincial government was formed, and liberation forces of the combined East Pakistani rifles, police regiments and young students vowed to rid Bangladesh of the West Pakistanis. Bengalis all over the world in the diplomatic missions of Pakistan began to defect.

Flying to England on the plane, I read the speech that Mujibur Rehman had given as he spoke to his people for the last time before he was arrested. My eyes were wet with tears as I finished it, and I prayed that God would give me, too, this kind of courage. Listen to a few of the words that he spoke:

"I am before you today with a very heavy heart. You know and understand everything. We have done our best, and yet the streets of our cities are drenched with the blood of my brother. Today the people of Bengal want freedom; they want to live; they want their rights restored.

"You elected the Awami League to frame the constitution. The history of the last 23 years is the history of the agonized cry of the people of Bengal; it is a painful history of giving blood, of the tears of an oppressed people.

"We gave blood in 1952. In 1954, even though we won the election, we were denied the opportunity to rule. By promulgating martial law in 1958, Ayub Khan kept us in bondage for ten years.

"In 1966, the six-point formula was submitted before the nation, and for this, many of my brothers were murdered. In 1969, in face of the mass movement, Ayub fell and Yahya came. Yahya said he would hand over power to the people, and there would be a constitution. We accepted his promise. You all know what happened after that.

"We had discussions with Yahya Khan, but he did not listen to me, although I am the leader of the majority party. He listened to Bhutto, who is the leader of the minority party.

"Bhutto came to Dacca. We had discussions with him. Our aim was to frame a constitution through mutual consultations . . . but Bhutto came out with threats. Yahya Khan postponed the Session of the National Assembly. The people of Bengal resented this postponement.

"I called for 'peaceful demonstrations.' But what did we get? Arms have been used against the unarmed people of Bengal. We have no weapons. The arms we bought, at our own cost, to defend the country from external aggression, are being used to kill my innocent people.

"Suddenly, without any consultation with us, and after discussions with Mr. Bhutto lasting five hours, Yahya Khan made a speech putting the entire blame for the developments on me and on the people of Bengal. While Bhutto was the guilty one, the people of Bengal were fired upon.

"Our struggle from now on is a struggle for emancipation, for freedom. There is a plot to finish off the people of Bangladesh. So please be careful. If they fire one single bullet, turn every home in Bengal into a fortress. You will have to face the enemy with whatever you have. If I am not there to give you directions, or if none of my colleagues are there for this purpose, you must continue to fight for freedom alone." (It seems he had a premonition of his imprisonment and the death of his colleagues.) "Bengalis have learned how to face death. Nobody can suppress them.

"Be on your guard. You should remember that the enemy

has infiltrated among us. They will try to create dissension among us under cover. Bengalis, non-Bengalis, Hindus and Muslims are all our brothers. It is our responsibility to protect them.

"There is a possibility of our living like brothers with the people of West Pakistan, if there is a peaceful settlement. If the Pakistan Army commits any more excesses we may never look at one another's face again.

"Be ready with whatever weapons you have in your hands. Since we have given blood once, we will give more, but Bengal must be liberated. This is a struggle for survival, for emancipation and for freedom . . . "

STANDING ALONE

Sigi told me later how that, as she was standing, watching me enter the plane, a great wave of loneliness swept over her. It was the first time for her to be completely left alone on the mission field. In front of her was a very difficult task. How could she accomplish it? But one thing filled her heart, determination to go through, no matter what!

She thought of the song I had sung for her in the meeting the day before, "You'll Never Be Lonely Again." Pushing her loneliness out of her mind, she said to herself, "I have a Friend Who will never leave me." Yes, He would go through everything with her. Had He not promised? "I will never forsake you, lo, I am with you always."

She turned to go back to finish her work for God, with expectation in her heart. But how would she ever get into East Pakistan? There was only one airline, the Pakistan International Airlines, flying into Dacca. Even then, there were thousands of business people waiting anxiously to get back to their families, for they had been cut off so suddenly and unexpectedly from them. All the planes which left Karachi for Dacca were carrying soldiers.

The next night she went to preach in a village. She preached hard, but her heart was a thousand miles away, wondering how God would perform the miracle of getting her to East Pakistan.

After the meeting, she spoke to a Christian brother who worked with the Pakistan Airlines. He told her, "Sister, there is no way to get into East Pakistan. The government has just passed a rule forbidding all foreigners to board a plane to East Pakistan."

Her heart was discouraged, and yet, she was determined to go whenever God made it possible. She studied the map to see if there was any other way to get into East Pakistan from the side, but there was none. East Pakistan was separated from West Pakistan by 1,200 miles. She was like a "madwoman!" She later said, "I couldn't even say why I wanted to go, but there was an indescribable fire burning in my soul, and I knew I had to go."

During the night of the fifth and sixth of April, Sigi was suddenly awakened. A loud voice was speaking, "You are going to see and tell the truth!" Falling on her knees before her mighty God, she knew He had spoken to her, and when He speaks, it must come to pass. Joy filled her heart. April fifth was the day when the West Pakistani troops ruthlessly murdered 300 members of the Awami League in East Pakistan. They were the colleagues of Mujibur Rehman.

The following day Betty Smith, the lady with whom Sigi was staying, came home from the market place excited. "Sigi, many of the missionaries have been evacuated out of Dacca and have arrived in Karachi." She went on to tell her that two of them, Charles and Elizabeth Oliver, had come into their place of ministry that day and told them about their experiences. "They have been through terrible things," she said. "I have invited them to come and stay with us to save their expenses, because they are living in a hotel and cannot afford it. So they will be moving in tomorrow."

Sigi's heart leapt in anticipation. She could hardly wait until they came, so anxious was she to hear the true news of what was happening in East Pakistan. For even though they read the newspapers and listened to the radio, the only news they got was what the West Pakistani authorities wanted them to know. Sometimes they managed to hear snatches of news from the B.B.C. station before it faded away. But the local news always said, "Everything is peaceful and under control." Now they would have the opportunity to hear the truth firsthand.

The following day, the Olivers arrived. They were obviously tired and worn out to the point of exhaustion. Mr. Oliver was very thin from fasting. His wife had dark circles under her eyes and was very pale. Sigi was introduced to them, and immediately she sat on the sofa, trembling with excitement to hear what they had to tell.

Slowly the terrible story began to unravel. They had been warned by the authorities before leaving East Pakistan not to tell a thing. "We have still more foreigners here and if you tell anything, we will shoot them," is what they had threatened. "Please," begged the Olivers, "tell no one what we will tell you."

On the 25th of March," Mr. Oliver began, with hushed tones, "curfew was suddenly announced. Most of the people had no radio and so they did not know about it. Those who had heard, didn't pay much attention to the report. The young people of Dacca were going to have a protest march. The army opened fire on them and killed thousands of students, professors, and teachers.

"They marked out the Hindu homes and started killing entire families. I went into some of their houses and found whole families of up to 14 members, from the youngest baby to the oldest grandmother, butchered to death. Blood often not only covered the floors, but flowed out onto the streets. There was no one to bury the dead, and the corpses were left to decompose, filling the air with the stench of decayed human flesh. It was just awful!

"Our church fasted and prayed for one month before it started, because we could see what was going to happen.

"There was such a panic in Dacca, that the people ran into the villages to find refuge there. The curfew was imposed for almost 24 hours of the day. If anyone went to the housetop to see what was going on, he would be shot by a sniper's bullet. Men or women going out to try to do some shopping were shot on the street."

He put his hand in his pocket and pulled out a bullet. "Look," he said. "Except for God's grace, we would be dead. We hid for hours under the table. This bullet entered the wall of our house. It just missed us.

"Many houses have been looted. One day a West Pakistani officer and his soldiers came into the home of a Westerner. He looked around at all they had and laughingly announced, 'I am going to take this record player with me to Karachi' and went out. Everyone knew that if they ever returned from whatever place they had fled to, there would be nothing left of their possessions." (Most of them would never be able to find even the slightest trace of their homes.)

"After the people ran into the villages in fear and terror, the army followed them, setting whole villages on fire. The simple straw huts burned easily and when the terrified people ran out of their burning huts, they were shot to death. It's impossible to believe," said Mr. Oliver, "that people can do such things."

Sigi had been listening, wide-eyed, to all this. Suddenly she spoke, "Brother, I have to go to East Pakistàn."

"What do you want there?" he asked. "It is impossible to have meetings because of the curfew. It is very dangerous for a girl, as they are raping many girls. Besides that, it is impossible to get in."

Sigi said nothing, but determination filled her heart to do all that God wanted her to do, even if everyone thought she was out of her mind.

The Olivers stayed a few days in the same house as Sigi. During this time, she learned to love and appreciate them. They were REAL missionaries, and not like many others who are without vision or zeal. Here was a couple who were more worried about their people than about themselves. They did not want to return to America nor did they want to stay in

West Pakistan. They too, had a burning desire to get back into East Pakistan.

"ARE YOU WILLING?"

On the 11th of April, while Sigi and her friends were sitting around the table having coffee and listening to the radio, they suddenly heard an announcement that the first flights were going into Dacca.

It was with great excitement that Sigi went to the meeting that night. "Brother," she said to her Pakistan Airlines friend, "I heard that the airlines are now accepting passengers for Dacca. Please help me get my ticket."

He was willing to go with her after the meeting to the airlines office. They went from one office to another, from ten o'clock at night until midnight. Always it was the same story. As soon as they saw her name, they said, "Sorry, this is a foreigner, and foreigners are not permitted to go to Dacca."

Sigi waited anxiously in the car outside, hoping that somehow they would overlook it.

At last, after the final attempt, her friend came out to the car. "Sigi, it's impossible," he said. "They always recognize your foreign name. The only thing left is to try to get your ticket for you at the airport."

The following morning, Sigi went to preach in the little church. Her friend was there, also. With a happy smile, he pulled the ticket for her from his pocket. He had managed to get one after all!

"Sister," he said, "you will be flying on Tuesday at nine in the morning. But you must wear Pakistani clothes, for if anyone recognizes you to be a foreigner, you will be in trouble."

From then on Sigi had a feeling of impending danger. She tried to push it from her, but when she heard on the radio that a Dutchman had been arrested and charged with spying, she wondered if there wasn't a possibility that she might be wrongly accused of her true motives for visiting East Pakistan. After all, who would believe that she went there only because she loved the people, and especially a people she had never even seen?

"I'll not worry about it now," she bravely said to herself. "There's time enough to worry if they catch me."

That night she fell on her knees before her bed. She had to talk to God. After a time, she became silent and listened. God was speaking to her. He was asking her a question. "Siegrid, how much are you willing to give for Me?"

"Everything, Lord."

"Siegrid, are you willing to die for Me?"

"Yes, Lord, but You said I would work with Sister Gwen in America."

"Are you willing to go to jail?"

"Yes, Lord."

"Siegrid, are you willing to die for Me?"

"Yes, Lord, but You have promised me I would have a ministry for You in America . . . "

"Are you willing to give up all that, and die for Me?"

This went on for about an hour. She knew that mere words and empty promises and vows were not enough. She had to mean it. She could be facing imprisonment or even death on the morrow.

She looked back over her life. She had lived 15 years under Communism. She had also lived in freedom. In either, she had not found satisfaction for her soul. Only the way of complete dedication to God was the way of peace and joy. Now the struggle with the flesh began. She was in her "Garden of Gethsemane" looking into the unknown and dangerous future, knowing full well it could mean prison, torture, and death.

"Lord," she wept, "I will drink this cup. Thy will be done in me. I will carry the cross You give me, no matter what shape or form it may be."

Suddenly, the great peace of God descended upon her. From her head to her feet, she was filled with this great peace, greater than she had ever experienced in her life, even greater than what she had experienced on the day she had experienced the saving grace of Christ in her life.

She got into bed and slept like a baby. When she arose in the morning, her hostess said, "Sigi, you look like you're going on a vacation trip."

After a good breakfast, they offered to drive her to the airport, but she refused their offer. She knew that on this mission, she had to go alone. She could not involve anyone else.

THE ARREST

Dressed in her Pakistani outfit of salwar and kurta, with a dupatta over her head, her eyes heavily made up to look like a Pakistani woman, Sigi arrived at the airport. She was early, but already the place was overrun with soldiers waiting to board the plane.

She was afraid to go inside the airport lest she be seen. Her friend found her, went to check in her baggage, and got her boarding pass while she waited outside.

People were walking by her on every side. It seemed that everyone was looking at her. Never had she felt so self-conscious in her life. Oh, for the power to make oneself invisible! It was true she was wearing a typical Pakistani outfit, but what about her face!

"Oh Lord, don't let them see my white face. You are a God of miracles, and it's not hard for You to do this," she prayed.

Anxiously, she waited for her friend to return with her boarding pass. At last he came. He had been successful. The strain of what he had done showed in his face. It was almost as white as Sigi's. Suddenly the realization of what he had done dawned on him. He not only could lose his job, and good jobs are hard to find in Pakistan, but he might be in even more trouble.

As he handed her the boarding pass, she felt a great respect for her Pakistani brother. He had risked a great deal for what looked like only a foolish girl's adventure.

"Sister," he said, "go with God. It is up to God now to bring you through," and he turned and left her.

With her new God-given peace still abiding in her heart, she walked into the waiting room. It was packed with soldiers and businessmen. There was great tension. This was one of the first flights for civilians into Dacca.

"Lord, don't let me appear to be ignorant of what to do. Help me to act as if I understand all the instructions given through the loudspeaker, even if they aren't in English," she prayed.

The first checkpoint she must pass through was guarded by armed soldiers. They looked right at her, but didn't seem to notice she was a foreigner. They looked at the boarding card and nodded for her to proceed.

Further along the hall was a second checkpoint, just like the other. Again she passed without difficulty.

Now came the most difficult part. She had to be personally examined by a woman especially assigned to this task. It was a security check of utmost detail. The woman called Sigi into the washroom. Passing her hands over her body, and then looking through her handbag, again she went through the ordeal undetected.

With a thankful sigh, she returned to the waiting room and sat down. By this time the other passengers had also passed through the security check and were quickly filing into the waiting room.

There was that one pale face among so many brown ones. "Dear me," she said to herself, "I hope I don't look like a sun in the night amongst all these people." She pulled her head covering down further over her face. Fortunately, no one came over to speak to her. Most were involved in their personal affairs.

Suddenly the door opened and a man walked in whom she knew. He also worked at the airport, but he did not realize fully what she was doing, nor the implications it might cause. He had just heard that she was leaving and he wanted to say goodbye, and because he had a special pass, he could get into the waiting room.

"Ah, there you are, Sister Sigi," he called out to her in a loud voice, and in English.

Sigi felt that everyone in the waiting room was looking at her. For a moment she wished she could drop through the floor.

"Not so loud, brother, please," she whispered, and wished him a thousand miles away.

But he didn't seem to realize still how dangerous a thing it was that she was doing. He sat down and started talking to her. Sigi was thinking, "How can I get rid of him, without explaining the whole story to him?" It was obvious he was not doing it intentionally, and to explain the whole thing to him here and now was impossible.

Fortunately, the problem was solved as the flight departure was announced. "Goodbye, I'll see you in a few weeks," she whispered, as she stood up, and hurriedly walked away to board the bus that would take her to the waiting plane.

There at the foot of the plane was all the passengers' luggage, waiting to be identified by the different passengers, after which it would be loaded on board the baggage compartment of the plane. She pointed to her suitcase. The attendant set it aside and without saying a word, she walked up the steps and entered into the plane. With a sigh of relief she took her window seat.

Slowly the plane began to fill. Every seat was occupied. She turned her face to look out the window, hoping she would not be observed. It seemed too good to be true. Sigi remembered her trip with me behind the Iron Curtain, and all the difficulties we had encountered that time. "It seems strange, but God surely receives more glory out of our problems and obstacles, than when everything goes smoothly," she thought to herself.

Just then, someone tapped her on her shoulder and asked, "What nationality are you?"

Looking up to see who was addressing her, she saw a handsome man in officer's uniform. "German," Sigi answered.

"Come with me, please!" he commanded.

As Sigi stood up to leave her seat, everyone was looking at her, wondering why she should suddenly be taken off the plane.

She came down the ramp. There she saw a jeep waiting for her. The thought came to her, "No wonder God asked me if I was willing to go to jail!"

It was with trepidation of what was about to happen to her, that she climbed into the back seat of the jeep, and was driven back to the airport. With a sinking feeling, Sigi watched the plane take off with her suitcase . . . on its way to Dacca.

The officer led her into a small back room and told her to be seated. Around her were gathered about five men, some sitting and some standing. They began to question her.

"Are you a reporter?"

"No."

"Where do you come from?"

"Germany."

They seemed to have the impression that she had just arrived, and therefore did not realize the situation. They asked to see her passport. But fortunately they did not seem to notice her date of entry, and that she had already been in Pakistan about two months. Had they realized that, it would have become much more complicated for her.

They questioned her for almost three hours. As she answered their questions, the words of Jesus came to her. "But when they deliver you up, take no thought how or what ye shall speak; for it is not ye that speak, but the Spirit of your Father, which speaketh in you." (Mark 10:19-20) So many of God's children had been helped and comforted by these words of our Lord down through the ages of persecution and martyrdom, and still they carry the same power to give peace and calm to the heart of the one who trusts in them.

And so it was, that no matter who questioned her, nor

how the question was put, Sigi answered with a great inner peace and calm which was so evident to her interrogators, that they were convinced that the mistake of permitting her to board the plane was their own, and they were so embarrassed that they had failed to stop her earlier, and therefore had unnecessarily caused her so much inconvenience. They gladly refunded her ticket with many apologies.

"But what about my suitcase, which has flown with your plane to Dacca?" she asked.

"We are sorry, but we can't promise to get your suitcase back for you from Dacca. The airport there is completely in the hands of the army, and there is much confusion there now."

After they were finished with Sigi, one of the officers asked her if she would accept an invitation to have coffee with him.

Gladly she answered, "Yes, thank you," because although they were finished with her, she was not finished with them. They walked over to the airport restaurant. When they were seated, he ordered coffee, and they started talking.

Before, he had questioned her. Now it was her turn to do the questioning.

He told her that he was a Muslim. His father was retired from a high position in government service.

"Tell me," she asked, with a smile, "how do you find me? I was almost in Dacca."

"It is your luck, I found you. I was looking through the tickets, when suddenly I saw your name, and I knew there must be something wrong. So I sent for you."

"What would have happened if I had gone to Dacca?" she asked.

"They would have shot you. Our soldiers are so angry with all the foreigners, they always come out of there and tell stories against us. If we find any who don't obey our orders, we shoot them. Why are you so anxious to go to Dacca? You couldn't really be going there just to see the place. Tell me the real reason you want to go."

So she told him. "I am a Christian, and as true Christians, we love our fellowmen if they are white or yellow, if they are Punjabi or Bengali. It makes no difference to us."

"How can you risk your life for those 'sweepers?' Those Bengalis deserve to be killed if they don't obey us. It is the only way. We don't want a split Pakistan. We will keep it at any price, no matter how many we have to kill or who oppose us."

"This is your point of view," she answered, "but with us, politics and customs do not separate us. We love each other through Jesus Christ. He makes us equal."

He shook his head in astonishment. This was too much for him. In silence they sipped their coffee.

After awhile, Sigi spoke again, "Please help me to get to East Pakistan."

The handsome young officer looked into the earnest face of this young German girl across from him, and something about her sincere appeal for help in those brown eyes touched his heart.

"I can't understand you," he said. "But I believe you want to go there for a Divine reason. I will try my best to help you. I know a very high officer in the army. I will talk to him about you, and I will personally do my best to get your luggage back from Dacca. May I take you to the place where you are staying?"

Sigi accepted his kind offer and he delivered her back to the door of the Smith household. The time was 12:30 p.m.

She was willing to die, and to go to prison, but she was not willing to come back a failure. Wasn't everyone praying for her? "What will they think of me now?" she asked herself. "Surely they will say I am only an adventuress, and that God never did speak to me to go; it was all my own foolish idea or things wouldn't have turned out like they did."

But then her courage returned. "What's the difference what people do think about me?" she asked herself. "Who am I trying to please, God or man? And He will surely make a way for me."

The next day the officer returned to see her. He brought back the suitcase, and he also brought her the news that he had spoken with his friend, and that there was absolutely no way for her to go to Dacca. "I wish I could help you," he said, "but I have tried my best and it's impossible."

Before they separated Sigi left with him her testimony of what Jesus Christ meant to her, and of His love for this young man. Only eternity will reveal the impact her love and consecration to God had on his life.

"YOU ARE GOING TO BE A REPORTER FOR ME"

Back in her room, she knelt to pray. God began to speak to her. "You are going to be a reporter for Me. Go to Calcutta!"

Calcutta, India is just 60 miles from the border of East Pakistan. New hope leapt in her heart. She had the key!

Three days later she arrived in Calcutta, feeling like a little lost chicken, not knowing where to go, or how to start. "Who," she asked herself, "will believe that I am a reporter?"

Just then the stewardess walked up to her and asked, "Are you a reporter?"

She was just going to say no, when she remembered what the Lord had said to her back in Karachi. He had said, "You are going to be a reporter for Me."

"Yes," she answered, smiling happily, "I'm a reporter for God."

The stewardess showed not the least bit of surprise. "Where do you want to go?" she asked.

"I don't know where."

"Well, you might as well get on the airlines bus and come into the city with us. There you can easily find a hotel."

After Sigi was seated on the bus, the fellow passenger across the aisle turned to her and asked, "Are you a reporter?"

This time she answered with still more confidence, "Yes."

God Himself had told her she was one, so she WAS one. Then she told the man about her difficulty and how she had tried unsuccessfully to get to East Pakistan from Karachi.

"The best thing for you to do, is to go to the Statesman Newspaper Office," he told her. "Theirs is the biggest English newspaper here and their reporters go behind the border all the time. They will be able to help you."

With this assurance, Sigi felt much better.

Within the hour, she had checked into a hotel, and was being pulled through Calcutta's mad traffic in a rickshaw to the Statesman Newspaper Office.

Never before had Sigi done anything quite like this. It seemed like an unseen power was drawing her on. It wasn't necessary for her to plan to do this or that; Someone was leading her, and she was simply following. In a few more minutes, she was sitting in front of the chief reporter, and telling him her whole story.

When she finished, he said, "There are two possibilities. One is that we have a girl reporter here from England. She is with the Times. She is a real daredevil, and is always doing the most dangerous things. You must try to meet her, but if she can't help you, then come back tonight. Then the press photographers will be back. They are just now returning from behind the border, and we are expecting them here tonight. They can help you."

However, after making enquiries, Sigi found that the woman reporter she was supposed to meet had already left, so she went back to the office to see if the men had returned from behind the border.

She was relieved, upon returning, to find they had arrived. When she told one of them about her desire to go behind the lines, he looked at her in amazement.

"I have just come back from there, as you know," he said, "and it is very dangerous to go there now. I was in East Pakistan many days. I went into villages and many places to find out the true story. I was born in East Pakistan, but when the partition came in 1947, I had to leave. So I know my way around there.

"While I was in one certain village, the West Pakistani army came, and I hid for three days and nights without food or water. That is how I got my pictures."

And then he showed her the pictures he had taken of war and terror, death and destruction.

As Sigi looked in horror on these scenes of terror, she asked, "Were you afraid?"

"Only a little. It is my work. I have to be ready always to die. Many of my colleagues have died in Vietnam," he answered. "But," he added, "for you to go there is very dangerous now. The army comes even over the border into India, and they shoot at the refugees. However, if you still want to go, and you have no one to take you, I will take you myself, even though I have finished my work. I will go once more for your sake."

Foolishly, Sigi asked, "Do I need my passports?"

Smiling, he answered, "You don't need one if they don't see you, and if they do see you, you won't need one either, because they will shoot you. Are you afraid?" he asked.

"No," she answered. "If you are not afraid to risk your life for your work, then I am not afraid to risk mine for my God."

Later Sigi found out that this kind man who offered to help her, was none other than Mr. Amiya Turafdar, one of India's most prominent press photographers, whose pictures have appeared in our leading news magazines.

The next morning Turafdar phoned Sigi and asked her to come to his studio. When she arrived, he told her, "Two hundred men and children have just arrived from Jessore, in East Pakistan. The best thing for you to do is to go there to the place where they are and get their story."

Sigi called a taxi, and after giving the driver the address, soon found herself in the slum area of Calcutta. The taxi stopped in front of a large building. A big crowd had gathered there. They had heard that the refugees had arrived and they all wanted to see them, but the big iron gates kept them out.

When Sigi alighted from the taxi, and paid the driver, she felt like one of the crowd.

"How will I ever get inside?" she asked herself. It seemed impossible.

Suddenly a man came to her and asked, "What do you want?"

"I have to go into this building, and speak with the refugees," she answered.

"Just a minute," he said.

In a few minutes he was back with another man. Sigi repeated her request. The man opened the big iron gate and Sigi walked inside.

There she saw, for the first time, the suffering of the refugees. He led her into a large room where about 200 women and children were sitting on the hard cement floor. In their fear and haste to escape, they had brought absolutely nothing with them, only their lives. Most of them were still in a state of shock. Some were crying; others were wailing loudly, as one wails for the dead in these lands, a sad and mournful cry that comes more from the soul than from the body. Others were just sitting there in silent despair and hopelessness. All had seen death and terror. All had escaped from a hell of man's anger and wrath.

"Please let me talk to one of these women," Sigi begged.

The man spoke to the women in Bengali. Out of the crowd, one of the women stood up and walked with them into an empty room. A mat was spread on the floor, and they all sat down on it together. Sigi's heart ached for the woman. She felt so limited, so helpless!

Sadly she asked her, "What happened to you?"

Tears started to pour down her cheeks. "I don't know. I can hardly even grasp it yet," she answered. "We never thought anything terrible like that would ever happen to us. We just wanted to live and have our peace, and we didn't pay much attention to anything that was going on around us. But one day the army came to our village. They came into our houses. They held their knives at our throats. They robbed us, and took away all our money and jewelry. We had to give them everything. Then they threatened to kill us. They drove all the women and children out of our village, but they kept our husbands and our beloved sons. We don't know what they did with them, whether they are alive or dead." Her body shook with her sobs of grief. There was nothing to live for.

Sigi tried to comfort her, and tell her that Jesus Christ had died for her, but the woman couldn't hear her, it seemed. Sorrow filled her face, her heart, and her mind. In silent despair she got up and walked out, with tears streaming down her face.

In one day, this simple woman who had never known anything beyond the affairs of her simple family and village life, had become an object of pain and hate. She didn't know if she would ever see her beloved husband and sons again. She didn't know if they were even then lying in their dried blood with their bodies decomposing in the little house that had once been the scene of happier days. Where was her husband now? Where were her sons? No one could tell her, or help her.

This sorrowing woman was one of not only 200, but of thousands who daily were crossing the border, fleeing with only their broken hearts and orphaned babies into India.

Alone, Sigi went back to her hotel room. There she prayed. She could not help that little woman, but she could speak to One who could.

The next morning, quite early, Sigi had a phone call. It was the press photographer, Turafdar.

"Sigi," he said, "come here to the studio."

Hurriedly, she got ready and went. The first thing he said, as she arrived, was, "Did you hear the story?"

"What story?" she asked.

"The story of what has happened at the Pakistan High Commission here in Calcutta. Ali Hussein has escaped into India, and has arrived in Calcutta. The High Commission here has declared its allegiance to the newly formed Sovereign Democratic Republic of Bangladesh. They have ripped down the West Pakistan flag and hoisted the Bangladesh one in its stead. From now on it's to be known as Bangladesh. They are forming a liberation army which will be trained in secret right in Bangladesh, and if it gets too dangerous, they will flee into India. Mr. Ali Hussein is confident that he is going to free Bangladesh from West Pakistan.

"Here are two reporters from Bombay. They are going to take pictures of Ali Hussein, and I want you to go along and interview him."

Sigi looked at him, startled. "Oh no, Lord," she prayed silently, "not that! I wouldn't know what to say to such a man. And on top of it, I don't have a reporter's card. I'm only a reporter for You, God, they won't understand that."

But before she could say anything, she found herself sitting in the car with the two reporters and was being driven to the Bangladesh High Commission. In her heart she hoped something would happen, that she would not be granted an interview. As they arrived in front of the building, there were crowds of people milling about. In their midst was a little table where a man was seated. He took all the requests to see the High Commissioner. She made up her mind that she would not say anything. If it were really God's will for her to interview the man, she would be able to get in, if it weren't, she would gladly accept the refusal.

After about ten minutes, they were granted permission to pass through the gates, and were ushered into the reception office to wait for an interview with Ali Hussein. She was wondering, as she sat there, what should she say to this important man? Never had she done anything like this in her life.

While she was waiting, a soldier from the Liberation Army came in. He told the reporters what was happening in Bangladesh. About a half-hour later, Sigi was called into the office to speak to Mr. Ali Hussein. She stepped into the room, and saw a nice-looking man with a kindly face, sitting at his desk.

With a smile he invited her to sit down.

Before she could think what to say, Sigi heard herself saying, "Do you know, sir, that the only help for your country is in God?"

"Yes," he answered, "I know that. Everyone is praying for God to help us."

"What has happened to the missionaries, sir?" she asked.

"Well, I can't say, but I believe that any who stayed behind, and fell into the hands of the West Pakistani troops have been killed. Doesn't anyone care for us? Must a whole generation be wiped out, and nobody lift a hand to help? Reporters are coming to the border and yet the truth is not told. They took 300 orphan children and three priests, lined them up in a row and shot them all to death. They took 700 women, starved them, raped them, and after seven days, killed them and threw their bodies on the street as a warning sign of what will happen to all who will revolt against their oppression. The people are dying by the thousands. They have nothing to eat. The only creatures that have enough to eat are the vultures and dogs who devour the flesh of our people. The vultures are so fat they can't even fly any more. When you return to your country, tell your people about the injustice. American bullets are killing our people, and yet, Americans don't know about it. You don't have to talk about politics, but please tell about the suffering of my people."

Before leaving, he told Sigi that the missionaries had done much good in his country and that when their land was free again, they would be welcome to return.

Sigi was then invited to meet Mrs. Hussein and one of their daughters, and their son. She sat with them and enjoyed a cup of tea together. They told her how worried they were about their relatives, as they had not heard any news from them. The daughter said, "I wanted to buy myself a dress, but after seeing the suffering of my people, and how my sisters have nothing, I can't spend any money on myself."

Deeply impressed, Sigi left. God alone had made the way for her to meet these courageous, beautiful people who had dared to take a stand against evil. Later she remembered how God had shown me He would use her to witness to and encourage some important person in government service. God's word is true.

TRIP TO THE BORDER

The next day, because the reporters were all busy, Sigi decided to go by train to the border by herself. After a four-hour train ride, she arrived at 1:00 p.m. as far as the train could go. Getting into a rickshaw she rode 20 minutes more until she arrived at the border hospital about which the reporters had told her.

When she entered, the head doctor told her that she needed a special permit from the army. Disappointed, she started out to look for the person who could give her this permission. She was sent from one officer to another, from one soldier to another, from one office to another. No one dared to give her the permission which she needed. But she insisted she must get into the hospital. She didn't want to make that long four-hour trip for nothing. Finally, a young officer drove her in a jeep to see the highest officer. After she told him her request, he gave her the permission without any difficulty and she was driven back to the hospital.

The head doctor met her, saying he would personally take her through the hospital. Before they started out, he said, "I hope you can stand what you are going to see. It is not like a Western hospital. We do not have enough doctors and nurses. Neither do we have sufficient medicine or blankets or beds."

Sigi confidently answered, "I am used to a lot."

But as he opened the door and they stepped into the ward, she thought her stomach would turn over. Sick people were everywhere. In almost every bed there were two patients. They were even lying on the floor. Some were screaming with pain. Their wounds were covered with flies. The small hospital had room for only about 50 or 60 people. More than twice as many were crowded inside.

As they walked from bed to bed, the doctor told Sigi that all of them came from one town. There were helpless children, women, young boys, and old men.

One woman especially screamed with pain. Her stomach had been slit open. Sigi could see that death was waiting for her. Others had gunshot wounds. There were little children whose eyes had been burnt out by chemicals. It was a scene of suffering and horror. Everyone Sigi talked to told her the same tragic story of terror.

When she was finished with her visit, the young soldier drove her back to the train station. She still had some time to wait before the train came. In the meantime, crowds gathered out of curiosity to see this white woman. Not many ever came to that part of the country. Soon, several hundred were crowded around her, staring at her. Sigi began to feel uncomfortable. The station attendant saw her plight. He kindly opened the door to the waiting room and she was able to sit inside until the train arrived which took her back to Calcutta.

AT THE FRONTLINES

Finally, the day for which she had been waiting arrived. Quite early on Sunday morning, Mr. Turafdar and Sigi started out for the border with another reporter. The car ride lasted about three hours.

Ten miles on this side of the border they could already see the continual stream of refugees coming across from Bangladesh. They didn't know where they were going. The unknown was their destination. All were looking for a spot where they could rest. Many were wounded, others were sick. Some had already died of cholera and many more would die before any vaccine was rushed to the border to inject the hordes of people running into India.

The border was heavily guarded. And only because she had come with these reporters was Sigi permitted to cross over into "no-man's land" and up to the front line. The soldiers warned them not to stay long. There was continual firing, and they could easily be hit at any time. The air was filled with the sound of gunfire, and the loud explosions of the heavy shelling.

The terrified people were running toward Sigi. As she stood there, she watched them fleeing with desperation in their eyes. Some fell on their knees and kissed the ground of India as they came across. The wounded left a trail of blood behind them from their bleeding wounds. Some never got any further than the Indian border; they died of their wounds after reaching safety. Fear alone had given them the strength to come this far.

The Indian Red Cross was at the border, ready to help the suffering. Scores of Indian doctors were later to volunteer their services to help the sick and wounded, but at that time, there were still too few, and the facilities and medicines were almost nil.

Sigi stood there with tears streaming down her cheeks. "Oh, God, what is this?" she prayed.

And God answered her there on the front lines of one of the world's most terrible and cruel wars that has ever been waged on this planet. "My daughter, you are tasting something of the end-time tribulation."

Then the soldiers made them return because it was too dangerous. It was impossible to go any further into Bangladesh, because the West Pakistani army was at the border and had captured the land right up to the border.

A few yards from the Bangladesh border stood a refugee camp which had about 8,000 people in it. Sigi and the reporter went up to the hut that stood at the entrance of the camp. Because Sigi didn't have proper identification, she was not permitted to enter. Mr. Turafdar left her there because he wanted to take some pictures.

Sigi sat watching the refugees walking by. Some had managed to bring out a little more. There were a few with oxcarts and oxen. A number had rescued their precious goats. There was a steady stream of humanity which slowly numbered from tens of thousands into hundreds of thousands until, at the end, ten million had fled for refuge into India, making it the greatest exodus in history.

Suddenly Sigi noticed a pair of black eyes piercing through her. They belonged to a young man who was wearing a dirty, torn white shirt and a doti (a long skirt which Indian men wear by wrapping it around their loins). There was a look of anger in his eyes.

"What do you want anyways?" he asked her. "All the reporters do is come and look at our misery, and then they don't help us anyway. And what is worse, they don't even tell the truth. Look at me! I am a student. Can you recognize it? I look like a beggar. All my friends were killed in Dacca. My mother, they raped; my father, they killed; where my brothers and sisters are, I don't know. But we are going to fight until we are free."

She assured him that she was not there because it was her job, but because God had sent her, and that she would not only give a true report to her people, but that she would also pray.

While she was still speaking to him, the director of the camp came and invited her to come inside the camp, and he personally led her through. Tears were running down her cheeks as he told her of the tragedy of Bangladesh. In the camp, people were standing with empty bowls in their hands, waiting for hours for a little rice. Many were sitting and sleeping on the bare ground without a mat, sheet, or blanket. No one had a second garment to wear. Worst of all was the hopelessness in their eyes.

Everyone had a story of tragedy to tell. One man had fled about eight days earlier. In the daytime, he hid, in the night he ran through the bush and jungle. One night he came to an open area. The full moon was shining. He saw what looked like bodies hanging on the trees around him. Looking closer, he saw, to his horror, the bodies of about 30 young girls hanging naked on the trees.

Many were the stories such as these that were brought out and told by the horrified people who had witnessed these scenes of violence.

As Sigi prepared to leave the camp, she saw a little refugee mother approaching the gate. In her arms she carried a baby. Two other small children on each side of her were hanging on to her skirts. When she got to the gate, she begged the gate-keeper to let her come inside.

"I'm sorry," he told her. "We are full. There's no room for you."

With tears of fear and despair, she stood and pleaded with him. Her children were weeping with fatigue and hunger and desperation, but the gate was not opened to her. Finally she gave up and turned to go. Sigi watched as she went a little further down the road, and then, sat down with her three babies in the dust by the side of the road.

Part Three

I was happy and relieved to see Sigi when she arrived in America. The story she had to tell filled my heart with gratitude to God for taking care of her and bringing her safely back home.

We began to minister in California and, as Sigi had promised the people of Bangladesh, she told the true story of their suffering. On the radio broadcast of the End-Time Handmaidens, we spoke about Bangladesh and begged our listeners to pray. At the same time we told how God had spoken to us to return with 12 women into the Baluchistan province of West Pakistan to work amongst the Pathans.

Many times I wondered who these 12 women would be. I knew they had to be women of courage and daring, women who loved God enough to make the sacrifice. Always we prayed that it would be the right ones.

One of the first volunteers was our dear friend and co-worker since the beginning of the End-Time Handmaidens, Dorothy Buss of Chicago. Dorothy is an accomplished violinist and a dedicated child of God. Three years earlier, as I had been seeking God in a lengthy fast, God spoke to her in the hours of the night, "I want you to join with Gwen in her fast."

At once she obeyed the Lord, even though she was a busy housewife and a mother of three sons. The result was that we have been joined together ever since in a fellowship and love that has united us to serve God. Since then Dorothy has travelled with me, ministering in Canada, England, Germany; and now God was leading her to come with us on our Pakistan-India tour.

The second woman who volunteered was Ruth Lutman of Santa Barbara, California. Her radiant ways and cheerfulness was a source of joy to us, and her service in End-Time Handmaidens' office was deeply appreciated.

One by one, women began to volunteer. The Lord had said that age was to be no barrier to going. The only requisites were a true love for the people and a willingness to lay down their lives if necessary. They also had to pay their own way. This meant great sacrifice. One woman had to borrow the money from a bank; another spent her life's savings. Three of them gave up their fine positions and good salaries. One had to leave college. The youngest was 18 years old; the oldest was 73. They were beautiful women, and I appreciate their love and sacrifice to God.

One day as I was preaching in Los Angeles I made the statement that if we had faith, we could have anything we wanted from God. I called the people who had a need to come forward and pray in faith, believing God for their miracle. Among the many who responded to the appeal was my son, Tommy. Tommy was almost 12-years-old at the time, and he had a beautiful child-like faith in God. Many times God had spoken to him in dreams and visions. As I prayed with the people, I also prayed with him and felt the very strong faith he had. I knew he was asking God for something big, and he was going to receive it.

After the service was over, he came to me and said, "Mummy, I am going to Pakistan with you."

I was shocked. "Son," I said, "it costs a great deal of money for you to go. Even Sigi and I do not have our fares."

"But Mummy, you said that if we believed, we could have anything we wanted from God, and so I came up and asked Him, because you said I would receive what I asked for. I believed what you said was true, and I believe God. I will go to Pakistan."

I could say nothing. Sigi and I looked at each other. I had been ensnared by the words of my mouth.

The days slipped by quickly, and it was nearing time to go. Sigi left ahead of us, so she could be in Germany for a few days. It had been decided that she would join our group in Rome. She only had enough money to get as far as Germany.

After she arrived there, she wrote me a letter telling me the wonderful news that God had met the need for her fare. The first miracle of supply had been met. Later we were to see how important it was that Sigi should have a different kind of a ticket than the rest of us who had an excursion ticket which limited the time we could spend overseas.

The date of our departure was October 4, 1971. We were to meet in Chicago, and go together from there. Two weeks before leaving, a gift of $600 came to the End-Time Handmaidens' headquarters. It was to be divided equally among Sigi, Tommy and myself. Sigi had used her part of it to fly to Germany. (Germany was enroute to Pakistan.) But the need was so great at headquarters and so many large bills needed to be paid before I left that I gave permission for the rest, which was meant for Tommy and me, to be used to pay the bills. A few days later, two of the ladies who were coming with us offered to pay my way. May God bless them.

It was a great relief to me, but I was having a problem with Tommy. He still was believing God would send him to Pakistan.

One night, after we came home from church, as he was getting into bed, he looked at me with a big smile. "Mummy, I'm sure I am going to Pakistan. God has given me two confirmations."

I sat down on the edge of the bed. "Tommy, I have something to confess to you. There is NO money for your fare."

"But what about the two hundred dollars that came for me?" he asked, in surprise.

"I'm sorry, son. I had to use it to pay bills," I answered sadly.

"But Mummy, it was for me!" He shook his head in elderly rebuke that made me feel like the world's biggest crook. "You shouldn't have done it."

"Tommy, I didn't only use your two hundred dollars, I used mine, too. Anyway," I added, "maybe it is better you don't go to Pakistan. You will miss school if you go."

"But if God wants me to go, He will help me to catch up."

"Tommy," I said, "if God wants you to go, it will need a big miracle. We are going in one more week, and we have to send the money in the next two days."

"Don't worry, Mummy," he said with a smile. "God doesn't need a long time to answer prayer." I kissed him goodnight and walked out of the room with a heavy heart.

Next morning when I called Tommy for breakfast, he said he wasn't having any breakfast. He usually has a very hearty appetite, and I immediately guessed what he was up to.

When lunch time came, it was the same story. Tommy said, "I don't want anything, Mummy."

"Are you fasting, Tommy?" I asked him.

He smiled at me, and his big blue eyes said "yes" with a twinkle, but he was too shy to admit it to me.

"Lord," I said, "what am I going to do with this boy? If he refuses to eat until the money comes for his ticket, he might starve to death."

I was truly becoming anxious. I wasn't even too sure it was God's will for Tommy to go. My mother's heart hated to see him miss that much school.

Sometime in the afternoon a dear brother gave me two hundred dollars which he said I could use for Tommy's fare, if I felt it was the right thing to do. Well, here was the beginning. But I didn't want to tell Tommy. We still needed about five hundred dollars. When it was time for supper, Tommy didn't even come around. He stayed in his room. A couple of times I saw him on his knees. That evening he insisted we go out and buy him a pair of hiking boots, so he could climb the Pakistani mountains.

Well, I figured, the boy can always wear boots. So we went out and bought them. He was very happy and proud of his boots. To his little heart they were a sign of a miracle to come.

About ten o'clock that evening when Tommy was asleep in bed, a lady friend called me on the phone. "Gwen," she said, "I can't stop thinking about Tommy. All day he has been upon my heart. I feel it is God's will for him to go to Pakistan and I want to help him. I will be receiving some money, about two hundred dollars, and I am going to give it to Tommy to help send him."

My heart leapt for joy. I knew now that God was watching a little boy fast, and God was working. I went to bed a lot more relieved than I had been for a long time.

"Lord," I said, "we only need three hundred dollars more. Please help us."

At 7:30 I was awakened by a long distance call. When I reached the phone, the friend on the other end of the line said, "I've been awake all night. I couldn't sleep. Last night I was digging a hole in my yard. I was hiding some silver coins I had saved, about five hundred dollars worth. It was dark, and as it was in the middle of the night, no one knew what I was doing. Suddenly God spoke to me, 'Why are you hiding this here, when my child Tommy is praying to go to Pakistan?' Sister Gwen, I must help Tommy to go. How much does he need?"

The tears rolled down my cheeks.

I hurried to wake up Tommy. "Tommy," I said, "I have good news for you."

He sat up in bed, rubbing the sleep out of his eyes. Putting his feet out over the side of his bed, he looked at me.

I said, "Tommy, you can go to Pakistan. God has given you the money for your ticket."

"Praise the Lord, now I can eat!" was his jubilant reply.

I told him the story in detail. He listened with a happy smile. When I finished, he shook his blonde head and said, "Isn't Jesus good!"

Tommy ate a hearty breakfast that morning.

THE COLONEL

When we were in California, Sigi and I had met a very sincere Christian gentleman who was a retired officer of the United States Air Force. For 23 years he had served his country.

I will never forget the first day we met Lieutenant Colonel James von Doornum Shaw. He was present at a Sunday morning Single Adults' Breakfast Fellowship at which I was speaking. The leader of the group pointed him out to me, telling me that he had been a high-ranking officer in the Air Force, and that in spite of his position he was a very humble and sincere person and a great Christian. She also added, "He is a Baptist."

That morning, as Sigi and I drove to the meeting, I had a strong feeling that God was going to speak to someone in that meeting, and that He was going to change that person's life.

As I spoke, I felt that my heart was being poured out. Someone was there who would meet God in a new way, and as a result, that person's life would completely change. I felt God was calling someone to a complete consecration.

After I finished, I asked them to bow their heads. Sigi went down one side of the room to pray for people, and I walked down the side nearest to where I was standing. One by one, we laid our hands on those seated there and prayed for them.

Finally I came to this man. I stood behind him and prayed silently. Scott and Carolyn Buss were playing the violin and piano. The room was filled with their sweet anointed music, "Sweet Jesus, Sweet Jesus, What a Wonder You Are!"

God's Spirit said to me, "Lay hands on him, I have a message for him."

"But Lord, he is a Baptist."

"Lay hands on him."

"But Lord, he will never understand."

"Lay hands on him!"

"But Lord, probably he has never even heard a prophecy before in his life."

"Lay hands on him!"

"But Lord, he will be offended."

"Lay hands on him!"

"But Lord, he will think I am nutty."

"Lay hands on him!"

I waited.

"Daughter, lay hands on him. I have a message for him."

I stood there praying silently, my head bowed.

"Daughter, I have a message for him. If you don't give it, it will be your responsibility."

At last I obeyed. As soon as my hands touched his shoulders I felt the mighty power of God going through me. His back was towards me. His head was bowed in his hands.

God began to speak His message to him through me. "God has spoken to your heart this morning. God shows me you haven't even begun to do the great things for God that you were born to do. God wants to bring you into a new place of consecration. You've got to let go of the things that have held on to you, and the things that have entwined you. Sell out to God. God will lead you into a new place in Him, a place of completeness such as you've never known, and satisfaction and joy. Completeness – that's what I see. Completeness. And from now on Jesus wants you to fall in love with Him as you have never been in love with Him. Even as you have flown in the natural, so shall you fly in the spiritual realm. There is a great high place in God where you shall soar upwards."

No one had told me that he had been a professional military and commercial pilot for 30 years, held an airline-pilot rating, and had flown many thousands of hours in over 50 kinds of military and civilian aircraft as a flight instructor, flight test and transport pilot. He might have been a "deskman" for all I knew. But God had known what he was! And through these words, God had touched his heart.

As the music faded, and the prophecy concluded, I walked back to my seat. "What a strange thing to say to a man like that," I thought.

It was true, Jim Shaw had never heard a prophecy before. He hardly knew what it was, but he knew God had spoken to him, and God had called him. From that day on, his life was changed. He began to seek God's will for his life. Like a small child, this great man wept before God, giving Him his life.

Later his mother told us, with tears, that when he was born she had taken this, her firstborn, and dedicated him to God's service. All these years she had waited and wondered when the time would come for God to claim him. In the years between, he had served his country with bravery and valor, but still, she knew the day would come when God would demand more of him.

And now, God, Who accepts every gift given to Him, had come down and claimed His Own.

Almost immediately after this, Jim went on a long fast. In these 28 days that he sought God with all his heart, God spoke to him and made a completely new person out of him.

Jim had heard about our plan to take 12 women to Pakistan. I could see that God was beginning to speak to him about this ministry. One day Jim told us that he felt it was God's will for him to come with us to Pakistan. "One man amongst 12 women!"

At first I did not consent. Sigi and I said, "Wait, brother, and see. We have to pray about that!"

As we were driving from Los Angeles to Chicago, God spoke to us that it was His will for His son Jim to go with us. And so we told him he should get ready.

When we gathered in Chicago to catch our flight, Jim was with our group. Later we were to realize how greatly we needed him, for he was a tremendous help in many ways, first as photographer, then in handling all the luggage, and last of all, in driving the women out to their stations. Truly God made no mistake, and neither had Jim, when he had heard the call to Pakistan.

WE BEGIN

It was an excited group of women who gathered at the Chicago O'Hare Airport on the afternoon of October 4, 1971.

"Is Ruth here?"

"Which Ruth?"

And well they might ask that question, for there were no less than three Ruths in our group. All three answered at once, waving their hands.

"Oh great! We were just getting worried you might have missed the flight in, or something."

"And there's Florence! Bless your heart!" We threw our arms around her and greeted her and the others with a happy kiss.

"But where is Rose?"

"She didn't get her passport in time, but she hopes to get it by tomorrow, and she will catch up with us somewhere enroute."

It was a one-stop flight to Rome, with only a couple of hours' break in London. I was looking forward to reaching Rome. I loved the city, and what was more important, Sigi would be there. That was the place we had planned to meet. I had bought a number of "happy pins" (the yellow pin with a smiling face), and we were adorned in our "badge of joy." Later I had many opportunities to be a witness for the Lord and leave a little joy behind as I gave away one pin after another to people in other lands.

At the Rome airport we were met by our tour representatives and whisked away to immediately commence our Rome tour. Time was short and we were not wasting any of it.

Coming out of one of the cathedrals, I suddenly saw Sigi standing there. She had been told by the tour people that we would be there and she had come to look for us. Wonderful! We all greeted her with joy. The only one missing was Rose Menken of Buffalo. Everyone was praying she would get her passport and join us in Athens.

When we gathered for dinner at our hotel in Athens, someone called out, "Sister Gwen, look who is here!"

And there was our Rose, smiling happily and as welcome as any angel that ever dropped out of heaven.

After five wonderful and busy days in Israel, we landed in Karachi, Pakistan, the land of our ministry. The beloved

Smith family kindly opened their home to us. The women slept on cots, on sofas, and on the floor. They were slowly being initiated into "missionary life."

The next day we boarded the train for our trip to Quetta. We started out the hard way, third class all the way – hard benches, no place to sleep. Some had kindly given their seats to women with babies, and so they stood much of the way. You never saw braver soldiers. None had been missionaries before. Most of them had never been away from their home- land. I wondered how long they would be happy and keep smiling in this jerky dusty train with its hard seats. I went over to sit beside Florence McCracken. She was smiling as blissfully as a girl who had just opened her biggest and best Christmas present and found just what she had always been wanting.

"How are you making out?" I asked her.

"Wonderful! This is my life. I couldn't be happier." You would have thought that she had been floating on a cloud.

After a long, tiring night, we were glad to see morning, but Florence never lost her smile.

The rest of us, who weren't so angelic, were glad to reach Quetta about ten o'clock in the morning. When the train rolled into the station we were greeted by Christiana and a happy group of Christians. They garlanded all of us with flowers.

We were happy to see our VW bus waiting for us at the station. A couple of years earlier I had been working in Ger- many. I had arrived there from India. One evening, shortly after my arrival, we drove to a meeting where I was speaking and noticed a beautiful new Volkswagen van. I thought in my heart, "This is what God's children need in India to help them to do His work." I remembered the Lord's words: "Every place whereon the souls of your feet shall tread shall be yours." (Deut. 11:24)

I thought to myself, "Why can't I claim this car?" In the dark, when no one was looking, I silently stood beside the car, laid my right hand on it, and claimed it for God's work in India. I never breathed a word of it to anyone.

Two years later, this car was given to me by the people of Germany, and my brother Earl and I drove it from Germany to India, where we were having tent meetings. When we finished our work there, I left it in Alice Shevkenek's care. She had used it in her ministry throughout India and Pakistan, and now, two years later, she had brought it to Quetta for our use in the mountains. I thanked God for it when I saw it standing at the railroad station, and asked God to bless the dear ones who had given it to us. It had gone tens of thousands of miles in service for God.

PRISONERS FOR A GOSPEL PORTION

The first few days were spent in preparation for going into the mountains. In the evening we had meetings in the city, and the women took part giving their testimonies.

Arrangements had been made for us to stay at Christiana's home, and also at the home of the Erickson's, our missionary friends who were at that time in Afghanistan.

Word came from Afghanistan that they were being held by the authorities as prisoners. Much prayer was being offered to God on their behalf, and we were all anxious for their safety. In the meantime, their home was made available to us for the use of our team.

One morning, shortly after our arrival, we were sitting in the garden when the gate swung open and our brother Erickson walked in. All of us were glad to see him and we immediately asked about his wife and three children who had all been in this great trial with him. When we were assured that the whole family was safe in Quetta, we indeed gave thanks to God, and bowed our heads in a prayer of thanksgiving. We were all anxious to hear the story of what had happened, so he told us.

"When we went into Afghanistan," began Gustav, "we took along a few scripture portions, because we knew that there is so little there of God's word, and it is illegal to print

God's word or any Gospel leaflets in Afghanistan. We wanted to share the truth of God with the people.

"One day we were in the market place. We were making some purchases in a shop. When we finished our business, we offered the proprietor a Gospel portion. There was another man sitting there in the same shop. He also asked for one. When he saw what it was he began to scream, 'Kaffir! Kaffir!' (Infidel! Infidel!) Which is what the Muslims call all non-Muslims.

"Immediately a big crowd gathered around. The man raved on about us, stirring up the crowd, until they became very unfriendly, and began pushing up against our little family. It seemed that our lives were in danger. We picked up the small children to hold them in our arms. Someone called the police.

"When we saw the police, we were very glad, because we thought they would help us. They took us to the police station. There we were asked to open our briefcase. When they found the few gospels we had in there they immediately became very angry with us. We knew we were going to have trouble.

"They shouted at us, 'Where did you get these religious books?'

"I told them we had brought them with us.

"This made them even more angry and they demanded, 'Don't you know it's illegal to smuggle them into our country? We have our religion. We don't want your foreign religion. You are a lawbreaker for propagating your religion in our country. We will have to hold you.'

"We had to stay in the hotel room where we were living at the time. A guard was posted at the door. My wife and the children were permitted to go out, but I was not allowed to leave my room except to be called to the police station for continual interrogation.

"Days lengthened into weeks and weeks into months. The hotel was charging us for our room and board. Our money was running out. It seemed like we would never get out of there. Those who held us were waiting for bribe-money to be offered them. The result was that we were held longer, with no hope of release in sight.

"Then one day a news reporter from a leading news agency who had come to Kabul happened to hear of our plight. Word was sent out to many parts of the world. People back in Norway and Sweden read about it and began to pray desperately. The attention of the world was being focused on the plight of our little family who were held so wrongly, and given so much mental suffering.

"The Afghans didn't want to become involved in what might well become an international affair, so we were released. We had been there three months. I was warned that I may never again return to Afghanistan, and was deported to the border. How thankful we are to be here! It's wonderful to be free again!"

This was the story Gustav Erickson shared with us. All of us were deeply touched when we heard about it. I wonder how many of us truly value our freedom and liberty, which it seems we are fast losing. Only after it is gone will we realize that, next to life and love, it is our dearest treasure.

MY PROPOSAL

The day before we were to go into the mountains, I called the women together. I spoke to them from Deuteronomy 20:8, "What man is there that is fearful and faint-hearted? Let him go and return unto his house, lest his brethern's heart faint as well as his heart." I warned the dear women of the dangers of the work ahead. I told them they may find themselves without food, maybe no place to sleep, and that the Muslims were often fanatically religious and could persecute or even kill them. Others had died for what they were about to do. I told them if any wanted to give up and turn back, that they could still do it in the eleventh hour.

But none of them wanted to return home. They had come this far, and they were ready to go all the way.

The women were divided into groups of two, each having an interpreter. Towns were assigned to them in which they would visit and work. They were told how many days to spend in each town. Jim, Gustav and Tommy would take one team to their area and leave them there. Then they would visit the second team, and after that the third team, until all six teams had been visited. If they found any of the teams were in difficulty, they would help them to the best of their ability.

The teams were:

No. 1 – Margaret Arland and Donna Riesen, both from California.

No. 2 – Ruth Lutman and Ruth Schimmick, also of California.

No. 3 – Ruth Glennon and Rose Menken, both from Buffalo.

No. 4 – Dorothy Buss of Chicago, and Florence McCracken of Niagara Falls, Canada.

No. 5 – Sandra Tresch of Buffalo and Sister Mae of Karachi.

No. 6 – Sigi and I.

Sigi and I chose what we thought would be the most dangerous area, the Afghanistan border. Christiana was our interpreter.

Some of the women had been sick with dysentery since their arrival. It doesn't take long to get it in these countries. But with great faith and courage they got up early in the morning, boarded their rickety old Pakistani "bus," and started a day's journey into the mountains. There were no toilets along the way. God had to do a miracle for them, and He did! As they went, they were healed.

After seeing the women off, Sigi and I and Christiana started out on our trip by another rickety bus for our destination. It was a never-to-be-forgotten trip for me. We three were the only women on the bus until about an hour out of the city. Then a woman got on board who was not used to taking the "back seat."

She squeezed herself down beside me, even though there hardly had been room for the three of us. That meant that four were sitting on one bench. At first I determined to give her as little place as possible, hoping that she would move somewhere in the back. But she was not to be discouraged. She wiggled herself into position and every time the bus bounced, she bounced herself over, giving me a big push with her bottom. Soon, I had almost no place left to sit.

I was becoming angry, and so I gave her a push back. Soon we were having "seat-war." I was trying to read a magazine. It had pictures in it. She reached over and grabbed it out of my hands and began to look at it. That was too much for me! I grabbed it back and rolled it up and gave her a playful "whack on the head" with it. She was angry now. She reached over and started to grab the back of my neck. I was beginning to think that things were going far enough. And I guess the Lord thought so, too. So He said . . . "Show love!"

Well, it was kind of a hard time to show love, but I tried. I put my arm around her and hugged her and smiled at her affectionately. This really threw her. She had never had anything like that happen to her before. She started to smile and let go. I breathed a sigh of relief.

Now she wanted to talk. She asked me if I had a husband, and how many children, and many such questions. When I told her I had three children, she wanted to know what they were. So I proudly told her, "Sons." Of course, this put me immediately up into a high bracket. In the Orient, if a woman has three sons, she is IT. But when she heard I had no husband, she began to feel sorry for me and said she would arrange a marriage for me. (Very kind of her, to be sure, but I wasn't interested. However, I thought it was a great joke.)

Then she said, "My brother is in the front there. He is rich and he would like a good American wife. I will arrange it for you." I looked to see which way she was pointing, and a big, husky, tall Afghan turned around and looked at me. He had a beard, black eyes, and the biggest nose I have ever seen in my life — and I've seen a few big ones in my day!

By this time the whole bus full of people were listening and they were getting very interested. My face was getting redder all the time. Sigi and Christiana were roaring with laughter.

She was getting quite enthused over her bright idea, and it appeared that the brother was becoming interested, also. I knew that "rich" in that country could mean an extra three goats and two horses. "We will make nice big wedding feast for you. My brother is very good man. He be good to you, lady," she said to me.

I knew that if she were as insistent about this as about getting my seat, that I was a loser. I thought desperately for an answer. At last I had one.

"How many wives your brother got?" I asked.

"My brother, he rich man, already got two wives, but he make you special wife."

"Oh no!" I said, trying to look sad at losing such a grand offer. "I no can marry man with two wives, must only have one. My country, only give one wife to men."

They looked at me in unbelief and shook their heads sadly. "Tut, tut, tut," she clicked. "Such foolish custom. In my country wife can take rest."

I was glad when we got to the end of the line and could get off. The last I saw as I turned to go quickly with Christiana and Sigi, was a tall, bearded Afghan, looking at me sadly.

OUR MISSIONS

It was dark when we got to our destination. We knew no one in the town and no one knew we were coming. We got off. In the darkness we had lost our lunch basket. After talking it over, we decided that the best place to find a bed would be the railway station. Usually they have a room there where the railroad employees can stay. We hoped we might be able to rent it for the night.

After getting there, we discovered there was an old servant in charge of the room. It didn't look like too bad a place to stay. With relief we put our luggage down on the veranda of the place and called the servant to open the door for us. But he only shook his head and told us we could not stay. "It is only for the railway people," he said.

When we begged him to please let us in for only one night, telling him it was late and getting dangerous for women to be outside, he got angry and shouted at us.

"You need special permission from the superintendent of the railroads," he said, and walked away, leaving us standing out under the stars.

"Lord," I prayed, "please help us! You know what it's like to have no place to lay Your head. When You came to earth, there was no room in the inn either; now, please give us a place to sleep tonight."

Just then we noticed a light. Two men were walking nearby carrying a flashlight. Christiana went over to see who they were and to tell them our problem if possible. To her amazement she found out that one of these two men was the superintendent of the railways. When he heard about our plight, he immediately gave us the necessary permission to stay and ordered the man who had locked us out to open the door and let us in, adding that the man must supply us with tea and bread, and such things as we needed.

We were thrilled to see how God had undertaken for us. But when we got our stuff inside and wanted to have a bite to eat after our long and tiring trip, we discovered that our lunch basket was missing. After searching fruitlessly, we decided we must have left it on the bus. It was too late to do anything more about it that night. We went to bed instead, giving God thanks for the miracle of sending the right man at the right moment. He told us that he never passed that way at that time of the night. "You are very fortunate that I came by now," he had said. "I never come here at night, but tomorrow at six in the morning I am going to Quetta, and I had a little business to attend to. That's why I was walking past."

We thanked God for doing all things well, and wondered what He had for us in this border town of Chaman, the gateway to Afghanistan.

The next morning Christiana went to see if she could find our lost food basket. While she was at the bus station, she saw a family getting on the bus with a very sick teen-age daughter. She immediately went over to talk to them and found out that she had been very sick for a long time. They were taking her to the hospital in Quetta.

Upon hearing this, Christiana said to them, "You don't have to make that long trip to Quetta. God has sent two of His handmaidens here, Sister Gwen and Sister Sigi. They will come to your house and pray for your daughter and God will heal her."

The parents were glad to hear the good news. They gave their address to Christiana and took their daughter back home.

When Christiana came back to our room and told us what had happened, Sigi and I looked at each other and started praying. God had to come through and help us now. This woman had "guaranteed" to the family that their daughter would be healed when we prayed for her. They could not be disappointed after that!

That afternoon we walked over to the place where this family lived. As we came into the area we found many needy people. We started going from house to house, talking to them about the Lord, praying for their sick, and leaving a word of cheer. They seemed genuinely glad that we had come and welcomed us in every place.

At last we came into the small hut where this little family lived. We saw the girl lying on the bed. She was so happy to see that we had come. The whole family was as joyful about our arrival as if we had been two angels. We walked up to the girl's bedside and started talking with them. The parents told us of the years and months she had spent in the hospital.

Our hearts went out to this lovely girl, so thin and sickly. We knew that unless God touched her, she did not have much time in this world. So we encouraged them in the Lord, telling how Jesus always loved the people and healed the sick, and that He had told us to do the same work which He had done. Then we prayed for her, and she immediately brightened up and began to feel better. It was wonderful to see the faith these simple people had in the power of God to heal their bodies.

The people invited us to have meetings with them, and so that night we had a meeting. A good crowd gathered and we told them the simple story of Jesus and His love and His power to forgive sins. We prayed for the sick.

They asked us to have another meeting the next evening, and so we again gathered in the open compound. God blessed these meetings in a wonderful way. Many testified how God had healed them. We walked back to our room at the railroad station late that night praising the Lord for all His wonderful works, and as we went, we left gospel tracts at many homes.

We also put them in cars and trucks wherever it was possible to do so. The people were sleeping. The streets were dark and still. We prayed that when they awoke in the morning, they would find this message of life and that many lives would be changed through it. The message on the tract was the one we had preached a half-year earlier in Sahiwal, "Is Jesus the Son of God?" It had been printed and thousands of copies were given out by our teams of women throughout this mountain area. It was a powerful message to the Muslim people.

When we finished our work in this town, we felt we should return to Quetta, rather than go on to the next town. It seemed to us that we should check to see how all of our teams were making out and then go on to the area which we were planning to work.

When we got back to Quetta, we found that one of our teams had been having difficulty. It was the "two Ruths" from California.

They had gone out bravely into the market area of their assigned place and began giving out tracts in broad daylight. The Muslim people became so angry that they called a meeting in one of their mosques to decide what to do with these two foreign women. They threatened violence. The local police officer found out about it. He took the ladies into his home for protection. When the angry men came to look for them, he protected and hid the women. Since the two girls could not go out on the street, they witnessed to the police officer and his wife, and had the privilege of leading them to the Lord.

When Jim, Gustav and Tommy arrived in their town, they found the women in the home of the police officer. He was very glad to have them leave the town safely. The men brought them back to Quetta.

After dropping them off at Quetta, Jim and Tommy went to the next area in search of Ruth and Rose. The men had left a message that they would return the same afternoon that we arrived. Seeing that they were supposed to return any hour, we decided to wait for them to take us to our next town; but they didn't come. We waited all afternoon . . . all evening . . . all night. I was becoming very anxious, fearing they may have had some trouble, maybe even an accident on those dangerous mountain passes. I knew Jim was a good driver, but, in these places the truck drivers take the whole road and cause many terrible accidents by their bad driving habits. I slept with one ear open, but no car drove up into the yard.

The next morning, we were all praying for news. About noon word came that Jim had phoned into Quetta. The car was broken down about 100 miles from Quetta.

I went with Gustav to the telephone office and called the telephone exchange of that town. A man there kindly got on a bicycle and drove out to the country where Jim and Tommy were stranded. He brought Jim back to the telephone office so that we were able to speak with him. It was a great relief to hear his voice on the other end of the line, but the news was not good. The car had broken down and it was impossible to fix it there. The only thing to do was to bring it back to Quetta. So I told Jim, "Try to load it on the back of a truck and haul it into town." It was impossible to tow it over those mountains.

Of course, one of my first questions was, "How is Tommy?"

"Tommy is doing great!" Jim answered. "He is sticking by me and using every spare minute to hand out tracts to all the passers-by. He chases after camel drivers, oxcarts, and bicycles. He is having the time of his life."

Tommy was a "born missionary." I knew this and so I was happy that he was about his Father's business.

They managed to get tea from a small shop by the side of the road. They had already slept two nights there in the car on the road, and unless they could get a truck to bring them soon, they would have to spend another.

When Sigi and I knew that they would not be returning to the city, and that they were in no danger, we decided to continue with our itinerary by bus. We went out the same day to another place.

The following day we went to a beautiful valley. The Pathans own this entire valley, and it is full of apple orchards, so I called it Apple Valley. We had a precious time that day and were not only able to give the Bread that came down from heaven, but we enjoyed some of those delicious apples.

When we returned to Quetta we were tired and hungry, so we decided to go to the one fairly good restaurant in town – a Chinese one – for a bowl of noodles. When we walked inside, we saw some of the women who had returned were also there. They apparently had gotten the same idea. And who was with them? Tommy! What a joy it was to see him! He and Jim had arrived a couple of hours earlier. They had managed only that very day to get a truck to bring them back.

Well, the van was back in the city, but it was impossible for Jim and Tommy to visit the two other teams now, so we prayed that God would guide them to come back by themselves when their work was finished. We waited a couple of days, and they, realizing that no one was coming for them, returned by bus.

The women returned with wonderful stories of the great things that God had done through their ministry. I want to share with you some of these experiences. What thrilled my heart most was that these were not veteran missionaries, or preachers, or evangelists, but rather ordinary women who might have been housewives, secretaries, teachers, etc. It proved to us that God's only requisite to be used is submission.

Submission can often be determined by a testing and proving in our lives. Sometimes this test can be quite severe. Dorothy Buss, who was not only a member of our team, but also an End-Time Handmaiden from the beginning, had to pay a price to be given this "call." She had heard the "call" of the Lord asking her to fast for 21 days, and after making this commitment and fulfilling these fasting days, God had begun to do wonderful things in her life. Now she was in Pakistan.

Then there was Florence McCracken. Florence had saved her earnings as a teacher over a long period of time. When she heard the call, she emptied out her savings account to make the trip.

One after another of these women made sacrifices. Submission is not difficult unless there is a price tag on it. But there are rewards that come with giving God our best. The greatest reward is to see God use you for His high and holy calling.

Dorothy and Florence came back from their itinerary with glowing reports of victory. When they arrived at their first station they found a fine place to stay. The caretaker in charge had graduated from a Christian school in 1926, but in spite of all the years that had passed, he still had a special place in his heart for the Christians, and for their Master, Jesus. He invited them to have meetings in his own home. He brought his daughter-in-law to them for prayer. She had been having internal trouble for a long time. Florence and Dorothy asked her to give them her charms, and then they prayed for her. God healed her immediately. After that miracle, their home was filled with people who came all day long every day for prayer. All of them were Muslims.

One day the caretaker gave them fish to eat. He said, "Jesus gave His people fish to eat, so I give you what Jesus gave."

The hearts of our women were deeply touched. They told of how fevers instantly left after prayer, and vomiting and dysentery ceased. One Muslim woman had been vomiting for 15 days and was in great pain. God instantly healed her. The people wept each time they left their area.

Sandra and Mae came back, faces glowing with joy, and told how that they had been in great difficulty with the authorities, but God had given them a wonderful door of ministry in spite of their problems. They had given away every last tract and gospel portion. People had said, "You have brought us the true Living Water." They had walked miles and miles, often working until midnight. God had healed everyone they had prayed for and again people wept when they had to leave.

Donna and Margaret came back telling how they had been so kindly received by the people wherever they went. God moved in a mighty way in the villages they visited also. People begged for more of the gospel records which we had brought along and which the people could keep because they were played by turning them with a pencil or sharp stick on a cardboard that had a needle. By some "miraculous" way, these records could talk when turned and the people spent hours playing them and listening to the message of salvation and the Love of God.

God bless the Gospel Recordings, Inc. and Joy Ridderhof, the great woman through whom this vision was born and carried out. They had given us large quantities of these records in different languages and the small cardboard players which reproduced the sound. I myself could never cease to marvel how so much came out of so little. These records, together with the tracts and gospels, were little "missionaries" which we left behind all over these mountains. Margaret wept as she told about one man who had followed them for 15 miles to hear the story of Jesus one more time.

Ruth Glennon and Rose had been in difficulty at their first place and could not do much, but in the next place they were joined by their interpreter and after witnessing and working, they also were able to come back with a report of having seen the Hand of God. Ruth was quite thrilled with her interpreter as he was indeed a fine man and very capable as a minister of the gospel himself.

Every one of the women said they would have liked to have stayed longer, and many wanted to return again. It is not easy to bring precious people to God and then to have to leave them without being able to help them know Him better. Many of the women told how kindly they were treated by the people and, although they suffered some opposition and persecution, the majority of the people were kind and good to them, opening their homes to the women and giving them the best food that they had, even though the women were strangers to them. One family even said, "Jesus has come to see us."

DANIEL

This story would never be complete without the beautiful story of Daniel, a young 21-year-old Frenchman whom we met in Quetta.

When we arrived at the Quetta station from Karachi, I noticed among the Christians who had gathered to welcome us a young, strange-looking character with long hair and a full beard. I wondered whether he was a "foreigner," or a Sadhu (a holy man). The light and smile on his face made me think he must be a Christian, and I found out soon that I was right. He was barefoot and dressed in Punjabi baggy pants and a long, flappy shirt. His name was Daniel.

We saw him in all of our meetings and, because he lived in the Erickson's house, our women were able to talk with him quite often. I began to get interested in Daniel one morning when I had the opportunity to talk with him and he told me some of his experiences. They were so beautiful and deeply moving, that I put him on two radio broadcasts that I was making at the time. This thrilled Daniel, because, as he told me later, he had always been interested in radio work.

Daniel was born and reared in France. When he was 18-years-old, he decided he wanted to see the world. His father and brother were atheists and Communists. Daniel was sympathetic towards Communism, but he was not involved in it so deeply. However, he was an atheist. To him, religion was all foolishness. He decided he was going to set people straight, and so he used to preach against God and the church. When he went to Rome he would get out on the street and speak openly against the Pope, God, and the church. Young people rallied around him and began to follow him, deeply impressed by his sincerity and logic. He spent months there before going on to Germany and Switzerland.

Although he had left home without any money, the miracle was that he was never hungry. People treated him kindly wherever he went, giving him a place to sleep and food to eat. He spent two months in North Africa where the Arabs in Tunisia, Morocco, Egypt, and Libya treated him kindly. They provided him with cigarettes, Coca Cola, and even shared their meals with him.

While he was in Morocco, he met a young 17-year-old Spanish boy who was also travelling about like he was. The two of them joined up and became good friends. They went on to Lebanon, Syria, Jordan, and Kuwait, hitchhiking their way to Afghanistan.

One day while they were in Afghanistan, a terrible thing happened. They had been smoking "pot" and were perhaps acting a bit strangely. This drew the attention of the young ruffians around there. They attacked them on the streets and started calling them names and throwing stones at them. One large stone hit his friend, Halvaro, on the back of his head. Daniel heard a loud crack! The next thing, he saw his friend holding his head and screaming with pain, running like mad. He managed to get control of him and the boy was calmed down but he was in agony for three days.

Every night he became delirious. One night Daniel found him standing at the window ready to jump out and kill himself. When the pain finally left him, he was mentally deranged: a lunatic. Daniel tried to look after him but it was almost impossible to control him. At first he wasn't so bad. He would just follow Daniel about, but later he got so unruly that he kept running away.

After eight days, they got a ride with some German people into Pakistan. The accident had happened in Kandahar and they came across into Quetta. In Quetta they found some Muslim people who felt sorry for the boy and they told Daniel they would look after him and try to send him back to his family. So Daniel, feeling he was all right in their hands, went on to India.

One day while he was wandering in a desert in India, he was thinking about all the strange experiences he had had so far, and he said to himself, "Nothing can surprise me now, except maybe I should believe in God."

The minute he thought that, a very bright light shone down on him and completely engulfed him. The power of God was so mighty on him that he began to weep. He had been seeking for truth in Hinduism, Sikkism and Buddhism, and now he knew God was right there, just where he was.

Shortly after that he was invited by some Christians to stay at a Christian Ashram (a guest home where seekers for truth can rest and be taught the dogmas of a religion). They gave him a French New Testament. As he read it, his heart began to burn like fire, and he saw that Jesus was not only a man, He was the Saviour of the world. He asked Jesus to become his Saviour, and a wonderful peace and joy entered his life transforming him completely.

Immediately he wanted to go home and tell his people what great things God had done for him, but he felt he couldn't go until he had paid some large debts that he owed. So one night as he was praying, the thought came to him how Peter had owed some money and Jesus had told him to go fishing, saying that he would find enough money in the fish's mouth to pay the debt. As he remembered the miracle that came through the fish, he said, "Jesus, why don't You do what You did for Peter? Why don't You put some money under my pillow, or better still, in my Bible, so that when I awaken in the morning, I will have enough to pay my debts so I can go home."

The next morning when he awoke, he looked in his Bible, and sure enough, there was a large amount of money in it, enough not only to pay his bills but to have quite a bit left over.

Thrilled with this new experience of what God had done for him, he had written his family. But they wrote him and answered, "You are very young . . . and foolish." They were used to his wild escapades and they figured this was just another of the same kind of thing.

With his debt paid, he began preparation for his return to France. But then, he started thinking about his Spanish friend and wondering where he was. Had he returned home? He decided to go to Quetta to see if anyone knew there what had happened to him. It had been three months since he had last seen him.

The first person he met on the streets of Quetta was none other than Halvaro. The boy cried for joy when he saw Daniel and said he had been waiting for him to come. He was still deranged, sometimes so badly that he didn't even know the beginning of the sentence that he had started to speak. Some Muslims were kind to him, but the majority made fun of him, mocking this madman and throwing things at him, teasing him and pushing him about. The boy was suffering terribly. He had lost his passport and was completely mad. It was a wonder that he remembered Daniel. The people who had promised to help him had not done a thing for him.

"Do you want to come home with me?" asked Daniel.

Yes, the boy was willing to go back home. So Daniel went looking for his passport, which he miraculously found in a hotel in the city. Because they had no visa to stay there, he went to the authorities with the passport, thinking they would have no trouble explaining their problem and getting an exit permit. But, when the authorities found out about it, they put Halvaro in jail. He was sentenced to one month, but because things go so slowly in those places, he had to stay ten days longer than the sentence demanded. Daniel was worried about him and often went to visit him. The boy could not speak anything but Spanish, and he was having a very bad time. They made fun of him and called him "Pagil! Pagil!" (Mad! Mad!) Daniel went to the judge to try to get his release, but because people wanted bribery money and Daniel didn't have any, the boy had to stay in prison.

During this time Alice Shevkenek came to Quetta for meetings. Through her ministry, Daniel received the Baptism of the Holy Spirit and learned to know God better. One day he asked Alice to pray for Halvaro. Sister Alice said, "Don't worry, God will heal him." They prayed for the boy, bowing their heads right there. Halvaro was 60 miles away in another town. At that exact time that they prayed, a miracle happened. The boy's mind was healed, his madness left him, and he was completely normal.

After his release, his family was contacted and friends helped him fly back to Spain, but Daniel was still in Quetta when we arrived. He was waiting for God to do a miracle so that he could go back to France. He wanted to return to the places where he had preached against God and tell the youth of this generation that he had been wrong. He knew he had been wrong because he had found God.

Today Daniel is working on the ship Logos, witnessing for the Lord in the Orient and whatever other lands that great gospel ship visits with its load of precious young people.

"SO THIS IS SHE!"

There was one more thing I had to do before I left Quetta. I had not forgotten the little Muslim woman whom I had seen on the plane the first time I had flown into Quetta eight months earlier. I wanted to see her. I had to talk to her. After all these months I had not forgotten this woman. Often I had prayed for her, whose face I had not seen, and I wondered what she looked like.

"Christiana," I said, "I must visit her."

She was afraid to have anything to do with the matter. "It's too dangerous," she warned me, "and that woman who could have helped you is sick in the hospital."

"Never mind," I said. "Just show me where she lives. Sigi and I will go by ourselves."

So Christiana went with us to the house, and then hurried away, because she didn't want to be there when we rang the bell on the gate.

An old servant with a cunning look on his face opened the gate for us. He asked what we wanted. I spoke to him in English and told him I had come to see the wife. He motioned us to wait there. Then he went inside the house and I knew he was speaking to the husband.

After awhile, he came out again. He wanted to know who we were, where we had come from, and why we wanted to see her. I answered all these questions, and said I had come with a gift for her from America.

Again he disappeared into the house. We stood outside waiting to see what would happen, silently praying for an entrance into that home of mystery.

After awhile he returned and told us we could come inside a closed area, resembling a screened porch, and sit there. About 15 minutes later, the door opened and the master came out.

"That's him!" I whispered to Sigi.

There he was! That tall, strange-looking powerful mystic, whom all the people feared. We stood to greet him. We prayed silently, as we were bidden to sit again, "God, even he can be shown Your love. Help us!"

"Where do you come from?" he asked.

"I'm from America, and my friend is from Germany."

Upon hearing this, he seemed interested. Obviously, he had

great regard for Germany.

"Why do you want to see my wife?"

"Because I have brought a gift for her."

"But why would you bring her a gift? How do you know her?"

"Sir, I know it sounds strange, for I saw your wife only once — when I flew on the same plane from Karachi to Quetta. She sat behind me. I felt such a love for her, I wanted to see her then, but was unable. So I purposed that when I returned I would bring a small gift as a token of affinity from one American woman to a great Pakistani lady. It is not much, sir, only a small gift of jewelry."

He seemed puzzled and surprised, as if he couldn't really believe me. But after questioning us for about 20 minutes, he said we would be permitted to meet her. We were then invited into a nicely furnished room.

He stayed with us, and we became involved in conversation. I found him to be a very well-educated and highly intelligent man. His relatives were connected with the United Nations and other great and powerful world government positions. The talk with him was most interesting and I felt the true compassion of God in my heart for him, which he, of course, could sense. He began to warm up to us and open his heart on the political problems of today.

Suddenly the door opened and a strikingly beautiful young woman, half his age, walked into the room, followed by a personal maid.

The shock of her beauty overwhelmed me. Her complexion was whiter than mine. She had rosy cheeks and raven black hair. Her eyes were like dark limpid pools of mountain water. She smiled graciously at us, showing a row of perfect, pearl-like teeth.

"My wife," he said proudly.

I acknowledged the introduction, still somewhat overcome.

"I have asked her to wear the Baluchistan dress for your sakes."

She was adorned in a brilliant combination of colours, exquisitely embroidered together.

"So this is she! This is what she looks like!" I said to myself. "Think of all that beauty hidden under those ugly black covers. What a shame!"

She began to speak. Her English was perfect (with a somewhat British accent).

I gave her the gift which I brought, a pair of pearl-and-rhinestone earrings for pierced ears. (All women in the Orient have pierced ears.) They were both very pleased, especially she, as all women love jewelry.

Tea and cakes were served as we continued our conversation. The two children and a baby girl, about one-year-old, whom I had not earlier seen, were brought in by their nurse to meet us.

The wife showed us her different national costumes while telling us they had given Mrs. Richard M. Nixon the identical kind of dress. When I expressed surprise, they brought out a family photo of President and Mrs. Nixon with their daughters Tricia and Julie, which had been personally signed by our President.

As wisely as possible, we shared the message of the love of God. When we at last stood up to leave, we found we had been there over two hours. Not in all this time had we been alone with her; consequently, we could not speak with her as we would have liked.

But they seemed interested in us and very friendly and hospitable. They invited us to visit them again when we returned to Pakistan.

As we walked out the gate, I was wondering, "Is he really as evil as people say? Or is this just the gossip of a superstitious and fearful people? Can he do all those signs and wonders?"

Close up, he had not seemed so bad. Certainly his wife had not appeared fearful of him. There was a big question in my heart about the whole thing, to which, even today, I still do not know the answer.

BANGLADESH REFUGEES

When the last team had returned to Quetta, our time was up. We took the train to Karachi and from there flew to Calcutta, India. We wanted to visit the Bangladesh refugee camps. Sigi and I also had hopes of going to the border again.

We had ordered 35,000 tracts to be printed and ready for us to distribute. They were the tracts God had given me for the Indian people and which He had so mightily used, "Who Is Jesus?" and a newer one, "Is Jesus The Son Of God?"

Within an hour after our arrival, the women were out on the busy streets giving out these tracts to the passers-by. They never wasted a moment to do something good for God.

Sigi and I worked two days getting permission for a carload of us to get into the Salt Lake refugee camp. It was near the Calcutta airport. In this camp there were 240,000 refugees, and another 60,000 were living outside the campground.

I will never forget the day we drove into that campground. I have seen many tragedies and much suffering in the 25 years I have spent on the mission fields of the world, but never have I seen anything that could compare with the sight that met my eyes that day. To see one beggar, or a hundred beggars, or even a thousand at a time is saddening to the heart. But, to see 300,000 gathered in one place, and to know there were one thousand more refugee camps such as these in India, completely overwhelmed me.

With tears pouring from my eyes, I walked along their muddy "streets." Most of them had only the clothes they wore on their backs. I saw not one sheet nor blanket in the whole place. Mothers sat on the doorsteps of their temporarily erected shacks and permitted their babies to suck their dry breasts as pacifiers for their hunger.

Men lined up for many hours to get a small ration of rice. Thousands were waiting at each distribution center. When it rained, they often stood knee-deep in water for a day at a time.

The greatest difficulty was sanitation. They had no shovels. How could you dig toilets? So the holes they had temporarily prepared were overflowing with human excrement. Flies carried disease from one pile of stench to another, and sat on the faces and eyes and mouths of the babies and children. The sick lay on the ground. In all their eyes was a look of hopelessness and sadness. No one wept when a loved one died. No one rejoiced when one was born; for each new one who came into the world was only one more hungry mouth to feed.

We visited the maternity center. A Franciscan priest, who was also a medical doctor, was in charge. The stories of desperation and sadness which he told us gripped our hearts. The fathers did not trouble themselves to come and see either their wives or their newborn babies. The mothers gave birth to their new ones in dumb silence and turned away from the fruit of their travail and labour, not wanting to see the child to which they had given birth. "Take it away," they would say. "I don't want to see it. It will only die anyhow. I do not want to learn to love it. Give it to someone who can care for it."

"None of the mothers ever smile," said the kindly priest. "That is the saddest thing of all. You just can't make them smile."

As we talked to the people, they told us of their suffering and how they had fled from their homeland. In very few cases did a whole family escape. Everywhere there were stories of terror and death.

The Indian authorities were not to blame for the condition of these refugees. The burden of a sudden influx of ten million was simply too great for India. It is hard to realize how many ten million people really are. It is more than the population of either Austria, Bulgaria, Cambodia, Denmark, Finland, Ghana, Iraq, Israel, New Zealand, Norway, Sweden, Switzerland, Uganda, Venezuela, or about 40 other countries of the world.

The Indian Prime Minister, Indira Gandhi, had said on May

24, 1971, "So massive a migration, in so short a time, is unprecedented in recorded history. They belong to every religion: Muslim, Hindu, Buddhist and Christian. They are not refugees in the sense we have understood this word, but are victims of war who have sought refuge from the military terror across our frontier. I am disappointed at the long time which the world is taking to react to this stark tragedy."

It was costing the Indian government millions of dollars. The total cost ran as high as 700 million dollars. Foreign nations proposed 200 million dollars in relief aid; but even if it is all delivered, it leaves a burden of 500 million on India, which is 100 million more than the foreign aid India receives yearly for development.

Daily there were 10,000 refugees streaming into India, and as Giesla Bond of the Deutsche Zeitung in Stutgart stated after an interview in a Calcutta camp, "Nowhere, not even in Biafra or Vietnam, has such tragedy been seen on this planet."

Quoting from her report, she said, "The wet rags sticking to the thighs, the blouses clearly showing the protruding ribs, the emaciated people had hardly the strength to drag themselves to the small village school which served as the Indian Receiving Center. A few collapsed during the last kilometer into freedom.

"Each of them was registered — name, age, profession, hometown. Like millions who had come earlier, they had to give an account and reply to the query: 'Why have you left your country, your village, your home?' "

"I do not have a house any more," said Nur-el Din, a young teacher from a place near Jessore. "Our entire village was burnt down by the Razakars army on March 26. The roving people's police had fettered all the menfolk of our district together and drove them to the market place. Among us were members of the Awami League as well. I, for one, do not belong to any party, but I am a Hindu. We had to stand in a line. A West Pakistani soldier raised up his pistol, with the cry, 'Traitors,' and shot down a few of those that were lined up. 'The others will be shot tomorrow,' he shouted. Two of my friends, themselves without any wounds, sank to the ground with their comrades who were shot down and to whom they were fettered. After a while in this hell, there came a non-commissioned officer who untied our fetters. They pushed us with sticks like cattle, back to our demolished houses. The dead remained where they were executed. We dared not bury them. No one knows where they were buried."

From the New Times came this report: "The face of Chandu Chandra was frozen in a mask of pain and despair. He spoke in a low voice, barely audible, as this young peasant recalled the night of horror that had robbed him of his all . . . family, home, country.

"Chandra was awakened that night by the rattles of machine-gun and rifle fire. 'Soldiers of the Pakistani army were combing the village, driving all the inhabitants into the common. The women were lined up separately. To commands shouted by a major, they were forced to drop down onto the ground and then to rise. For hours mothers and sisters were subjected to this senseless torment, but we could do nothing to help them; the soldiers had rifles. The troops went through the rows of women, tearing off silver bracelets, necklaces, earrings, the modest ornaments handed down from mother to daughter. Then they bound us up and led the women into the houses, and from there cries for help, screams and groans smote our ears . . . '

"Blood and ashes were all that remained of this native village after the cutthroats left. Chandra, who narrowly escaped with his life, fled into India."

From all over came stories so tragic that the retelling of them is almost repulsive, yet the story must be told and I will tell it as it was told to me. Listen, reader, and know that this is indeed the beginning of the tribulation.

"Along with the wholesale massacre, our women are being subjected to unspeakable brutality, including rampant physical assault. Rape of women of every age, their sexual organs cut to pieces as the victims die screaming, pregnant women having their unborn babies bayoneted inside their stomachs, infants snatched away from their mother's arms and thrown into flames, young children being thrown up in the air and then spiked with the bayonet as the body falls. . . .

"Women were lined up, the more beautiful were chosen to be used by the officers and the lesser by the jawans (enlisted men). They were taken to the camps where they were stripped totally naked and whipped at the slightest expression of unrest. There they were tied to the bed posts and other places where they were continually raped by the men. Many died. Others became mentally unbalanced. The pregnant ones were thrown out to suffer shame and disgrace so great that they wished themselves dead.

"An old woman and her 20-year-old pregnant daughter, Batisha, were walking towards their home about two miles from the local police station. On the way the Pakistani soldiers beat the old woman and took away the girl. Two days later, the girl was discovered dead. Her body carried marks of the most brutal kind. Beside her lay the unformed body of her still-to-be-born child."

The story could go on and on. For when so many millions die, you must know that the brutality is beyond the power of the pen to describe.

While we were in Calcutta, Sigi and I visited again the Bangladesh High Commission. Mr. Ali Hussein was out of the city, but we had a very good visit with his wife and daughters. They gave us an interview for our End-Time Handmaidens broadcast. The lives of these beautiful teen-age girls had been deeply affected by this tragic war. They told us how, in their home, they had kept one girl about ten years of age. She had seen her father murdered. She had been forced to watch it happen. The effect of the tragedy was such that she became a nervous wreck. She used to faint for apparently no reason, many times a day. And at night she would have nightmares in which she relived the scene and would awaken the house screaming, "Don't hurt my daddy! Please don't kill him! What has he done?" And she would scream until some-one would come and calm her.

"Was her father in politics?" I asked.

"No. He was a simple farmer."

And so the innocent died and their children suffered, and the world looked the other way and said, "Am I my brother's keeper?"

From Calcutta, I took the women to Delhi, and after a day in this city and in Agra, where they saw the famous and beautiful Taj Mahal, we flew to America, leaving Sigi behind. The women would never again be the same. Our mission was accomplished, but for Sigi the most difficult part of her work lay ahead. I knew the task she had to perform was very hard but I had confidence in her, for she had proven herself to be a real "soldier." However, the situation was daily becoming more tense as soldiers were massing along the borders of West Pakistan and Bangladesh on both sides for what looked like might become an all-out Pakistan-India war. It could break out at any moment. I was glad to get our team safely back into America, but Sigi would be left behind to taste more of the "End-Time Tribulation."

Part Four

As we prepared to leave Delhi, it was a sad Sigi, already feeling the pangs of loneliness, who watched us pack. Five o'clock in the morning found us boarding the airport bus that would take us to Palam. She stood outside the Y.M.C.A. Tourist Hostel sadly waving goodbye. Already she felt lonely.

She was flying that very day to Kabul, Afghanistan. In her purse was a list of the spare parts she needed to purchase there for the VW van. Buying the parts there was less than half the cost of buying them anywhere else.

After the last goodbye was waved, she slowly turned and went upstairs to her room. She was alone. After you have been with a crowd for a long time, you feel the aloneness that much more.

Her flight wouldn't be leaving until noon so she had ample time. She felt like praying, and as she prayed, her "Best Friend" came and stood by her giving her His sweet peace and courage so that she could begin her new task with boldness. It was good that she did not know what dangers lay ahead.

It was getting dark when she arrived in Kabul. She had to find a place to sleep in this strange city. I had left her all the money I had, but still it was very little. After the motor parts were paid for, she would have almost nothing left over. So she looked for an inexpensive place to stay. It was not too difficult to find one. Everybody was friendly to this lonely girl and gave her advice which suited her pocketbook.

The next day she contacted the Johnsons, a Swedish couple who worked with the United Nations. They invited her to visit them. They were very gracious and friendly people and Sigi immediately felt at home with them. They told her about the difficulties the Christians in Afghanistan were having in trying to spread the Christian faith. Missionaries were not allowed in Afghanistan. Those who wanted to do any type of missionary work had to come in as doctors or technicians, etc. There was a church, but it was mostly visited by the foreign community. Afghans could only come in secret and dared not tell anyone because their lives would be in danger. They are not permitted to own Bibles either, so they often kept their Bibles at the homes of Christian friends.

Just a few days before that, a missionary who was visiting Kabul went into the mountains with a friend to pray and meditate there. They parked their car and climbed a high hill. After their time of prayer was over, they went back to their car.

As they were about to drive away, a man standing there suddenly pulled out a gun and shot the driver in the head. She was dead instantly. The car began to move, and gaining speed, started rolling down the mountain with the missionary inside. It was impossible for her to stop it before plunging over a cliff. She managed to crawl out of the wreckage, but was badly injured.

Stories of murder and intrigue were constantly being told. In one month alone, 12 young people (mostly hippies) were buried. Some had died of typhoid fever and others of tuberculosis. And there were those who had been found on the streets with their heads cut off.

It was not good for Sigi to live alone in a hotel, they told her, so they invited her to come and stay with them. After hearing these stories, Sigi was very happy to accept the invitation and the same afternoon they helped her move over to their home.

Sigi felt much better living with them. Now she had someone with whom she could share her problem of how to obtain the parts for the car. After discussion, it was decided that the best thing would be to purchase the spare parts at a garage where there was a German engineer who could help her and thereby she would be more sure of getting the correct materials.

The following day she went to the garage and talked with

the man. He gave her the price list on all these parts, and to her chagrin, she found the prices much higher than we had anticipated. She realized that if she bought the parts, there would be very little left for her living expenses. She went home to pray about it before handing in the order. No one could advise her what to do. She had to "hear from heaven."

That evening the Johnsons were visited by two young Afghan men. They had discussed Christianity with Mr. Johnson and were very interested in hearing more about it.

Over a cup of tea, they opened their hearts. They were college students. It was the month of Ramadham, during which the Muslims fast for 30 days from sunrise to sunset. Most of the Muslims are very strict about keeping this fast, either out of religious principles or fear of displeasing others. But some of the students with more liberal ideas did not want to follow the old traditions and they started to eat.

Soon a group of fanatical students got together against them and there was rioting between the two groups. The Muslim priests were especially angry, and thinking they were doing God a favour, they cut into small pieces the student who had dared to eat. Obviously the young men expressed fear to break away from the Muslim religion to become believers in Jesus Christ!

The following day, Sigi returned to the garage. She had decided to go ahead and make the purchases. After all, she reasoned, the car was not for anyone's personal use or pleasure, but rather for the Lord's service. The German man promised he would have everything ready for her the next day.

The next problem was how to get everything across the border into Pakistan. Sigi had very little money left and some had warned her that the duty could be as high as one hundred percent. At first, it seemed that the best thing would be to find someone going by car from Kabul to Pakistan and go along with them. However, nobody wanted to go because there was danger of war between Pakistan and India breaking out any day. It seemed impossible to bring almost a whole motor across the border by bus. Sigi was sure they would see the parts and demand duty, and since she had no money to pay the duty, they would seize it all. This meant she would lose over $300 worth of equipment. She went on her knees to find the answer from God, and once again He spoke to her heart. "My daughter, don't you think I can protect you the same in the bus as in the car?"

That was right! God was in control of the whole situation. She knew what to do. She would go by bus!

The next day she picked up the spare parts. She could hardly believe her own eyes. There were so many things. Where would she put them? How would she pack it all? She hurried back to the house. The bus was leaving in a little while.

First, she emptied her suitcase, trying to find a place for it all. Then the thought came to her, "Suppose they forgot something. I'd better check these things with the list."

It was a good thing she did. One of the most important parts was missing. It was impossible to get it that day: the shops were already closed. Reluctantly she returned the bus ticket and bought another for the following day. It seemed like the day had been wasted because of a careless mistake.

Because there was not sufficient room in the suitcase, she bought another, a leather one made in Afghanistan. Now there was space for everything. The crank case went into the newly purchased suitcase and most of the other parts were packed in the Samsonite. It was so full it looked like it would burst, and so heavy she could hardly lift it. This was not good. So she took it all out and started to pack all over again. Finally the job was done and she was closing up the new leather case. Just then she heard a strange sound, and looking, she saw there was a big tear in it, and the crankcase was sticking out. In weariness and desperation she just put a towel over the whole thing and left it as it was. If the customs official looked into it, she would be in trouble, but she took comfort in knowing God had said He would protect her the same by bus as by car.

"IF THEY CATCH ME . . . THEY CATCH ME."

The next day Mr. Johnson drove her to the bus station. It was waiting to leave. People were loading all their luggage on top of the bus. When she saw that, Sigi thought, "That would be a good place to load it, for surely they would not bring all that heavy baggage down for inspection. She placed the big, broken bag beside the suitcase. The smaller bag which contained the four cylinders she was going to keep with her in the bus so it would not be broken. She had just nicely seated herself when Mr. Johnson said, "I'm sorry, Sigi, but they will not put the leather bag on top. You must keep it beside you on the bus."

It was carried in and dropped down beside her, crankshaft sticking out and all. The bus driver started the engine. A goodbye wave to Mr. Johnson, and she was on her way over the Khyber Pass, across the border, and into Pakistan.

"Well, I might as well enjoy the scenery," Sigi reflected. "If they catch me . . . they catch me. But God can make a way then, too." She leaned back and started to relax.

Beside her sat an elderly German lady. She was about 48-years-old, dressed like a teen-aged hippie, and having a great time living a hippie life. It was interesting hearing her tell of many adventures and strange experiences. She told Sigi she was on her way to Ceylon where she planned to spend a year. Apparently she had hitchhiked her way all across Germany, Austria, Bulgaria, Turkey, Iran and now Afghanistan. Sigi marvelled at her. While they were talking, Sigi noticed there was a man sitting in front of them who kept looking at her. She was getting annoyed with the special attention he was giving her and decided to ignore him, hoping he would leave her in peace.

In spite of her cold attitude, he smiled at her and kept trying to converse with her, only to be continually rebuffed by her. Meanwhile, they were getting closer and closer to the border. The last miles seemed so long, but at last they arrived.

Going out of Afghanistan was no difficulty, everything went smoothly. But when the passengers piled back into the bus to proceed to the Pakistani customs and immigrations, the bus wouldn't start. The driver tried and tried, but all to no avail.

Finally, the people all got out and walked to the Pakistani immigrations. After they came out, they saw the bus had been driven up in front of them. At last it had started and the driver had been able to drive it in front of the customs house.

Men were unloading the top of it. Everything came down, Sigi's suitcase included, and all was carried into the customs building. Sigi knew that this was the hour she needed a miracle, and as she watched, she saw it take place in front of her eyes.

Although they had brought in her Samsonite, they had forgotten the other two bags which were inside the bus. Sigi began to hope for a miracle.

As the customs officials stepped up to inspect her suitcase, she noticed that the tall Pakistani man who had been trying to talk with her earlier was standing beside her. All the officials were treating him with utmost politeness, as if he were a very important person. She realized he must be a very influential and well-known man. She began to wonder who he really was. Just then, the customs official said to the gentleman, "Is she with you?" meaning Sigi.

For some strange reason, he answered, "Yes."

"Well then, we don't have to look in her suitcase," the official said.

"Yes, look," he answered the official.

"Please look," added Sigi, unlocking and opening it up very bravely, while her heart was praying he would neither see nor feel anything.

As the suitcase lay open in front of her, she leaned herself over on it, covering the parts. She looked at the official. He looked at her. "What material is this suitcase made of?" he asked. "It looks like good stuff."

"Yes," she answered. "It is a good American case."

"Shut it!" and he helped her tuck all the edges in, and held it down till she had fastened down the locks. He then called the porter to take it and put it back on the top of the bus. When the porter tried to lift it, he was hardly able to do so, it was so very heavy.

The customs man smiled and said, "It's as heavy as if there was iron in it."

"That's right," answered Sigi, smiling even more. "It sure is!"

Now Sigi really wondered who this strange gentleman was. She had to find out. When he spoke again to her, she answered him and soon they were conversing. To her utter amazement she discovered he was no small personality. He was a businessman just returned from abroad. He usually flew into Pakistan, but he had missed the plane the day before, and so he had decided to come by bus, a thing he never did. And on top of all that, he was related to President Yahya Khan.

Sigi's heart was full of thankfulness to God. Now she could understand why she had been delayed another day. Surely all things work together for good to them that love God and are called according to His purpose . . .

Sigi began to witness to him about the Lord. He, being a very zealous Muslim, tried to convert her to the Muslim religion, while she tried to make a Christian out of him. The conversation ended in a deadlock. Before they went their separate ways, he assured her that Yahya Khan and Bhutto would never give up East Pakistan at any price.

When they reached Peshawar, she found a fairly good hotel. Leaving her luggage in the room, she went to the railroad station to enquire about train schedules. To her dismay she found that the train journey to Quetta took 36 hours. Considering the condition of trains, it was like a little eternity of misery and discomfort. There was only one train a day. The train had just left, and the next one was scheduled to leave at 8:00 p.m. the following day.

The next afternoon Sigi decided to go out to the market to

purchase some fruit for the long journey ahead of her. When she stepped out on the street, she was suddenly surrounded by rickshaw pullers and beggars. They all crowded around her, shouting for attention. Tired from her travels, all the noise and confusion bothered her; so rather than push her way through the crowd, she stepped back into the hotel, sat down at a table in the warm sunshine and ordered tea.

She hadn't been sitting there ten minutes when the assistant manager came over to her and took the chair beside her. She groaned inside of herself. She didn't feel like talking to anyone. But he wouldn't allow himself to be ignored.

She looked at him. He was a handsome man with beautiful white hair — old enough to be her father. But his eyes were not those of a father's. They gleamed with lust and unclean desire. She shuddered and prayed, "Lord, be with me."

"I like you," he said. "I am lonely. Come into my room; I want to love you."

Sigi was both shocked and angry. "I'm not interested, sir!" she answered him. "Don't think that because I am alone, you can approach me in such a way as you have."

"But," he argued, "I'm lonely. My wife is not here . . . and I love you."

"How can you love me? You don't even know me. It is not love you speak of, but lust and unclean desire. Please let me alone!"

"No," he answered, "I'm not going to let you alone. I'm going to keep you in the hotel and not let you go," he threatened.

"If you do that, I'll call the police," she answered.

Thoroughly upset with the whole affair, she stood up and walked into her room leaving her barely-tasted tea on the table.

Back in her room, she fell on her knees and cried, "Lord, I feel so cheap and degraded. If I didn't know that You are with me, I wouldn't be able to travel alone." Soon she felt the strength of the Lord flowing into her soul, refreshing her. She read her Bible and prayed and in a short time began to feel better again.

"Thank You, Lord, for speaking to me, encouraging and helping me. I know You are always with me and will not fail me. I praise You for these trials which bring You close to me."

She ordered another pot of tea.

The waiter came with the tea tray and placed it on the table in her room. He saw her Bible on the table.

"You Christian?" he asked in broken English.

"Yes," answered Sigi.

"I Christian, too. I live in busti. If you need help, I help you."

He was like an angel of the Lord to Sigi. They started talking, and soon she found that he knew people whom she knew.

"Do you know Sister Gwen?" asked Sigi.

"Yes, yes," he said. "I hear her preach."

Now Sigi felt truly at home. How wonderful is the fellowship of children of God!

"I work with Sister Gwen," said Sigi.

He got very excited when he heard that and his face lit up with joy. Now Sigi was truly comforted. God had sent His child to her at the right time and the right place.

That afternoon she boarded her train with a much lighter heart. The manager had not dared to trouble her again.

Sigi had a seat in the women's compartment of the train. She was surprised to find it was empty, an almost unheard of thing in Pakistan. The next compartment, however, was quite crowded. She was hoping some other women would join her, but none came. After awhile, the door opened and eight or nine young men got on the train. They sat down all around her. It is never permitted for a man to be in the women's compartment. She anxiously searched their faces to try to ascertain what kind of fellows they were, and whether or not she would have more trouble. They were looking at her, too, as curiously as she was watching them.

"You alone?" one asked.

She nodded, "Yes."

"Not good!" he said. "You danger. You no sleep. If you sleep, people come steal everything. What country you from?"

"Germany."

"Oh, Germany!" he smiled. "Germany very good."

"Why?"

"Germany have good leader. Number one. Adolf Hitler. If we have him, we beat Indians for sure. Anyways we beat India. Pakistan army number one."

Sigi was amazed at the hatred these young men felt toward their Indian neighbour. The strangest part of it is that most Pakistanis have relatives in India. Until the partition in 1947, it was all one country. How dreadfully the hate-propaganda can subvert the minds and thinking of man, until he thinks he is justified in hating and killing his own brothers and sisters.

After awhile, one of the fellows asked, "Tell me, is it true that European and American people lay all day in the sun to get brown skin? I can't believe it."

"Yes," answered Sigi. "It's true."

"That's crazy. We stay out of the sun because we want to be fair and they stay hours in the sun to get brown." He shook his head in disbelief.

Handing her a stick of sugarcane, he asked, "Here, you like sugarcane?"

She accepted it and started to chew on it. It tasted like sweet wood to her, but after a bit of hard work, some juice was derived from it, and it didn't taste too bad.

When the train reached the next station, the fellows jumped off, and she was left alone. In the next compartment the men were talking and she wondered what the night would bring. She placed all her cases on the top bunk, and crawled up into the one opposite it. In this way she could watch it better. It was December, and the night air was cold. Besides, there was a draft blowing through the train. She had not been able to bring any blankets. While in Kabul, she had bought an inexpensive sheepskin coat. It had a terrible odor, but it was warm, so she wrapped herself up in it and hoped for morning.

Every little while she could see eyes looking at her. Men were coming over from the other compartment. She pulled her head scarf over her face, hoping the others would think she was a Muslim, as they treat their own women with much more respect. It looked like a bad night was ahead for her. Her only trust was in Jesus.

She must have dozed off awhile. Suddenly she was wide awake hearing voices near her. Maybe someone was trying to steal her suitcase. She jumped up quickly bumping her head on a fixture. There stood two men with guns, staring at her.

"We watch you!" they said.

"What do you want?"

"We police. We looking for dope. You got dope?"

"No," she answered, shaking her head.

"Good!"

Everything was quiet for a while. Suddenly one of them interrupted the silence. "You want peanuts?"

She took a few from the small bag he held out to her. One of the men sat down on the bench and stared at her.

"Very dangerous. You alone," he shook his head. "You sleep. We watch."

She was thankful for these two guards, but she didn't trust them either. After a couple of hours one of the soldiers got up to go, calling the other to follow him. He seemed reluctant to obey. He stood up and looked at Sigi. Suddenly he reached out and took hold of her hand. "You come with me."

"No," she shook her head emphatically. "I have to go to Quetta."

"Come with me!" he begged again. He could hardly speak any English, and she didn't know exactly what he wanted but she knew what she wanted to do, and she certainly wasn't going with him. The other soldier called again. The train came to a full stop. He turned and left her to follow his comrade.

It was around 2:00 a.m. Again she started to fall asleep

and was awakened by somebody shaking her arm. She opened her eyes to see two more soldiers standing looking at her, more terrible looking than the first.

"Open your suitcase!" one of them commanded.

Sigi looked at the time. "What?" she scolded. "At 2:30 in the morning? Why do you bother me? What do you want?"

"Dope."

"I have no dope."

"Open your suitcase. The other day we put two Germans in jail. They had smuggled a whole suitcase of hashish into Pakistan from Afghanistan."

She tried to convince him she had no hashish, but he insisted on searching her case, so she climbed down from her bunk.

"What will happen if he finds the parts?" she asked herself. She could not lift the suitcase down, it was so heavy, so she climbed up, and opened it. He climbed up and searched inside.

"What's that?" he said, pulling out a car part.

"Part for my car."

"What car?"

"I have car in Pakistan. I want to fix it with that."

The answer seemed to satisfy him. Then he wanted to see the other bag which had the crankcase in it. But by now she was determined he wouldn't look inside, in case he got too smart.

"Ah . . . " she said, "it's way up there. It's too much trouble to take down. I don't have dope."

"Leave her alone!" the other soldier spoke up. "Never mind. Let's go!"

Finally they left and she was alone again. Troublesome as the soldiers were, at least they had frightened the men in the next compartment.

The next time Sigi opened her eyes, it was morning. Daylight was coming in the windows and the car began to fill up with some women. Relieved, and weary with travel, Sigi ordered some breakfast from the station restaurant. But after eating, it made her sick. So now she also had to suffer with an upset stomach for the next 26 hours.

At Lahore, the whole compartment filled up with women. She was a real attraction for them – the only white woman amongst the crowd. At first they were shy and kept talking about her to each other while watching. Although Sigi was feeling miserable and sick, their chattering and inquisitiveness made her smile.

Lunchtime came and they all pulled something out of their bags to eat. They noticed that she ate nothing. When evening came and the same thing happened, they began to get worried about her. Up till then, they thought she was observing the Muslim month of fasting, but when the sun went down, and she still hadn't eaten, they decided to feed her. With dirty hands, they handed her rice and chapati.

She shook her head and pointed to her stomach. They smiled knowingly and one after another came and offered her a cup of their tea. Even though it wasn't very clean, she accepted it gratefully.

Night came again, but this time she felt better. There was safety in numbers. Even the longest hours passed, and at last, the train arrived at Quetta. When Sigi saw Christiana's kind face at the railroad station, she was happy. She felt like she had come home.

FIXING THE CAR

It appeared that war was imminent and that very little time was left. Everywhere were seen signs which read, "Crush India." The troops were leaving for the front lines, and the whole atmosphere was one of tension and fear. Sigi wanted to finish her job as quickly as possible so she could leave and get home to Germany. We needed her in Germany. Our church was waiting for her there. And yet there was a job for her to do in Pakistan. Sometimes it seems as if one of us is not enough.

But before leaving, she had to have the car fixed, drive it

out of Pakistan, and re-enter it again, as it was in the country on a carnet, and the six months allowed for its stay had nearly run out. Neither was it possible to get an extension. It would have meant losing the car if something was not done about it. The authorities are very quick to seize any vehicle that is not properly in order. When they confiscate it, it is next to impossible to get it back.

Everyone was warning Sigi to be careful about who fixed it.

"You can't trust the garage," someone said. "They steal the new parts and put in old ones, and because you are not a mechanic, you wouldn't even know the difference."

Sigi knew anything was possible. She remembered the story a man in Afghanistan had told her. He had taken his car into a garage in Pakistan for an oil change and checkup before driving it to Afghanistan. Later that same day he picked it up. When he got to the border, the customs officials checked his carnet. As is their custom, they always look to see if the serial number on the motor agrees with the one on the carnet. To the utter amazement of the man, they found that it was another number. On closer inspection, he found there was a completely different motor in his car – one much inferior to his original one. He realized that the garage must have taken out the original motor and installed a completely different one when he took the car in for the oil change. The customs officials didn't believe his story, nor did they show mercy. They seized the car and there was nothing he could do to get it back.

Sigi was thinking about this story, and wondering what to do. Christiana suggested having the car fixed in their yard while they watched it being done. This was a good idea, but where was the mechanic who would do it? Sigi still was sick with a bad cold, and in a cave of confusion. They couldn't reach a decision.

One day they decided to take it to the garage. The next day they felt they should not. Meanwhile, the days were slipping by and nothing was being done. It was all very frustrating. "Oh, if only there could be one brother I could trust, who knew something about these things!" Women seem so helpless at times like this.

Confused, troubled and anxious, Sigi fell asleep. That night she had a dream. She saw a railroad crossing signal, the old kind they used to use in Germany. When a train is coming, the signal is down, meaning to stop. When it is up, it means all clear, and one can proceed. In the dream, the signal was up. Sigi took this as a sign from God that she should start to have the car repaired.

The same day, a young man named Peter came to see her. He said he would fix the car for her. She didn't know if she should trust him either. Looking at him, she asked, "Do you know anything about Volkswagon motors? Are you sure you can fix it?"

He spoke with assurance.

She thought, "Well, if I can't trust him, I can at least trust the Lord," and she and Christiana decided he should do the job.

The next day he came with his tools and Sigi took a chair and sat down beside the car to watch and pray. She prayed, "Lord, help him to put that motor together correctly!" Then she watched to make sure no parts were switched.

While the car was being fixed, they looked for a reliable person who could go with Sigi across the border into Afghanistan. It had to be someone with a passport. This made it difficult.

Finally, one day Peter said, "I have a passport. I can go with you if you get me a visa."

This made Sigi happy. Who could be better than the man who fixed the car? If something should go wrong, the mechanic would be on board! It was much too dangerous to go alone. Everyone knew the terrible story of what had happened to the English woman . . .

She had travelled that same road some time before. Nobody knows why she had been travelling alone, but they all knew what had happened to her. Someone had kidnapped her and taken her up into the hills. There she was raped, killed, and her body thrown over a cliff where she was later found. They never did find the person or persons who did it. And by the appearance of some of the wild-looking characters in the area, there was more than one who looked capable of repeating that same horrible act.

Now Sigi had a man whom she felt she could trust. She took his passport and hers over to the Afghan consulate. She had no trouble getting her visa, but when the man in charge looked at Peter's passport, he shook his head. "Sorry, we can't give him a visa."

"Why not?" asked Sigi.

"Pakistanis can only go into Afghanistan once a year," he answered. "And he has already been there once this year. Not until next year," he added, handing the passport back to Sigi.

"But, sir," begged Sigi, turning her big brown eyes on him, "please have mercy on me. I need him to help me go there and back. He fixed my car and I'm not too sure it will work. If it breaks down, I will be in danger and much trouble. You wouldn't want anything bad to happen to me, would you?"

He took back the passport, opened it up to a clean page, and without a word, stamped a fresh entry visa for Afghanistan in it.

"Thank you, sir," said Sigi, a big smile lighting up her face.

It was a happy girl who came walking back to the compound of Christiana's household, but when she saw the engine still in parts lying around and time so quickly passing by, she became quite frustrated.

Sigi later told me, "I never felt so much anxiety about repairing a car. It was like an expectant mother waiting for her baby's arrival." Like everything in this part of the world, it takes longer than anticipated. There are always unexpected delays.

But at last, after another week, the motor was all put together. Now came the crucial moment. Would it start? Sigi and Christiana stood beside the car with anxious faces while Peter attempted to start the motor.

Nothing happened!

"What's wrong?" cried Sigi.

"I don't know," said Peter. "Maybe it's the starter. It should work."

"Let's push it."

So they pushed it. Still it didn't start. It was as dead as a pile of junk.

"No! No!" groaned Sigi.

"Let's get a jeep and pull it," suggested Peter.

The jeep was engaged and they tied the van to it. Down the street they went, while Sigi and Christiana stood watching with their hearts in their throats.

Suddenly they heard a sputter, then another, then a roar. The engine was running!

"Praise the Lord!" they exclaimed with upraised hands.

Proudly, Peter unfastened the car from the jeep and drove it back to the house under its own power. There WAS a God in heaven after all! And He knew how to fix motors!

INTO AFGHANISTAN

Before going across the border, they felt they should test the motor. So the next day they drove to a nearby town about 20 miles away. The car worked fine there and back.

"Good!" said Sigi. "Now we can go to Afghanistan."

She was in a hurry to get this part of her responsibility over, so they decided to leave the same afternoon. If all went well, they would be there within three hours.

Christiana and Riaz, the young man who had been Dorothy and Florence's interpreter, went along for the ride as far as the border. They would return by regular bus transport, as neither had passports.

By the time they left Quetta, it was already late afternoon. The road led over mountains and through valleys. Khojak Pass is said by some to be the second highest mountain pass in the world, 7,750 feet, second only to the famous Khyber Pass, which is north of it.

They had gone only about 15 miles when the car stopped on a hill. Not until they pushed it did it start again. Then Sigi smelled something strange. It was like rubber burning. No one else noticed it for a while, but finally Peter said he could smell it, too. The lights of the car went out.

They stopped to investigate. By now it was dark; however, there was a full moon. It was a beautiful, cold night, but an awful place to be broken down. No one had a flashlight. Peter crawled under the car, and with the aid of matches, he searched to find the trouble, while Sigi and Christiana prayed. He found a fault with the electrical wiring and tied on another wire. The lights went back on permitting them to continue their journey.

By now it was midnight and they had come to the foothills of the mountains. Peter said, "We will have to take the military road. It is more dangerous, but not so high. The car should not climb so high right after an overhaul job, it's too hard on the new motor."

They came to a road which was blocked off. Peter honked the horn but nobody appeared. Then two men moved the roadblock away and they drove through. Fortunately it was a bright moonlit night, as it was a terrible road — much worse than the other one. On one side were towering mountains and on the other side, sheer cliffs dropping straight down two to three thousand feet or more. There were no road signs or markers of any kind to guide the driver. The road itself was wide enough for only one car to drive on, and even then, it was broken almost completely away in places leaving only a black, gaping hole into nothingness. Only by clinging to the side of the mountain could they get through these dangerously narrow passages. Christiana was hanging on to the seat in front of her and praying as loud as she could.

As terrifying as the situation was, Sigi had to smile. Sometimes there is humour in tragedy. At last they started coming down the other side, one hairpin curve after another. Their ears were hurting, but it was a good feeling for now they knew they soon would be over the worst part of the way.

It was 2:00 a.m. when they drove into Chaman, the border town. The border would not be open until 9:00. Where should they go? It was too cold to sleep in the car. The men wanted to sleep at the busti, but Sigi and Christiana knew that if they went there, excited people would want to visit and they were too tired to talk. They also knew it was too late to stay at the railroad station. Hotels? There were none! This is the same place Sigi and I had been only about five weeks earlier. It seemed like a year had passed since then. The only thing left for them to do was to stay at the Roman Catholic church. They stopped in front and Christiana pounded on the door of the keeper's hut. He opened the door looking grumpy and sleepy.

"May we have a room to sleep here, sir?" asked Christiana.

"No. I can't give you a room. I have to ask the bishop."

"God alone knows how many hundreds of miles away the bishop is," thought Sigi. But she knew where "her Bishop" was, and she called on Him to soften the man's heart.

Christiana stood firm. She had one foot in the door and, being a woman, she knew how to beg.

At last, after 15 minutes, he relented, and they were shown a room with two empty beds. With thankful hearts they opened up their bedding and sleeping bags and crawled in to sleep with all their clothes on.

The men had already driven to the busti, looking for a place to spend the rest of the night, promising they would pick them up early in the morning.

They awakened after a few hours, took a little "cat-wash," drank a cup of tea, and waited for Peter and Riaz to come. But they didn't arrive. There was no place to sit, so they walked outside and waited there. Sigi began to wonder what was hindering them. She leaned against the wall and started to pray. Suddenly she saw a vision. The Volkswagon was involved in an accident. As suddenly as the scene came before her, it vanished.

"No, it couldn't be! I must be imagining it," she said, pushing the thought out of her mind.

They waited another half hour, and then at last, the men came. Both were looking pale and cast down.

"I'm so sorry," said Peter. "We just got hit in the side by a big truck driven by Pathans. It was entirely their fault. They drove so close to us, they scraped the whole side of us where the door is."

Sigi and Christiana went around to the other side and looked. Sure enough, there were the big, ugly marks of a bad sideswipe.

"When they hit us," said Peter, "they stopped and got out. As soon as they saw it was a foreign car, they said, 'Oh, it's a foreign car. It's not our fault. It's always the fault of the foreigner.'"

What could Sigi say? Surely God had prepared her for it by warning her ahead of time. So she just thanked God that it had not been worse.

As they started on their way to the border, Peter told how he had slept last night in the car to protect it. "It would not have been safe to let it stand outside unattended in this place," he said.

When they arrived at the Pakistani border, Riaz and Christiana left them to return home. Sigi and Peter continued alone. They had no difficulty crossing both borders, except that every time the car stopped, the engine stopped running and they had to push it to start it again. This was pretty annoying with people standing there watching them.

The distance from the border to Kandahar is about a hundred miles and, with all going well, they arrived there in the early afternoon. Kandahar was a small crowded city full of bicycles, carts, horses, camel caravans, and hundreds of pedestrians. In the midst of the traffic the car stalled. Soon they were surrounded by the curious crowd who gathered around to look at Sigi. Besides that, there were the usual beggars, money changers, and dope peddlers. Everyone tried to make business with them.

"Let's go right back," said Sigi. "Do you think we can make it back to the border before it's closed?"

Peter looked at his watch. It was 3:00 p.m. "I think so. If we hurry."

So they pushed the car, got it started, and drove back the way they had come. When they arrived at the Afghanistan customs, the officer examined their passports. Peter stayed outside to watch the car.

"I'm sorry, I can't let you go through. You don't have a stamp from the police station in Kandahar," the officer said to Sigi as she stood waiting outside.

"Since when do I need a stamp from the police?" she asked.

"Yes, you do. You must go back to Kandahar and get one."

Then suddenly he said, "Come. I'll check your car and inform the immigration police and let them decide what to do with you."

He went over to the car and searched it thoroughly, then went back into the building. When Peter wanted to follow him inside he commanded him to stay outside. By now it was obvious to Sigi that he was detaining her purposely and that he wanted to be alone with her.

She saw the time was going quickly and soon the border would be closed.

"Hurry, sir," she said.

Slowly he picked up the phone and dialed a number. He put the receiver back down, saying, "The phone is broken. I can't get through. You will have to stay here."

There was a second officer there, but he was no more helpful than the first.

"Please sir, you must help me. I have to get across the border before it closes," begged Sigi.

"If you'll help me . . . I will help you," he replied with narrowing eyes.

"You want some money?" asked Sigi.

"No."

"What do you want?"

"I like you. I want you, girl." His eyes were filled with

lustful hunger.

Fear crept into her heart. Her mouth went dry. "Lord," she prayed, "I know You are going to get me out of this situation, but I wonder how."

"Keep calm, and ignore him," the answer came.

She pretended not to understand him.

He insisted his offer was fair and square. If she came into his back room with him alone, in a little while she would be free to go.

Sigi ignored his offer and talked about something completely different, still pretending she didn't know what he was talking about. In the meantime, she looked out the window hoping someone would come and rescue her, but nobody came. Except for Peter, who was forced to stay outside, the place was deserted. The man had her passport and she was at his mercy. In a little while they would lock up for the night. Already, it was getting dark. She knew unless a miracle happened, she would be forced to spend the night here. She waited. The minutes ticked by, a quarter hour, a half hour, 45 minutes. "Oh God, help me," she prayed inside.

She had to sit and wait. He was waiting, too, for her to break down.

"God only knows how many other foreign girls he has abused and bribed with offers like this. But this time he has one who won't be bribed. I have God. Perhaps the others didn't. That makes a difference."

A whole hour went by. He looked at her with a mocking smile. She looked straight back at him, praying.

Peter still was outside. By now he was getting worried but he knew he couldn't go inside.

Suddenly the man picked up her passport, stamped it, and told her she could go. She took it and walked out quickly.

When they came to the immigration office, she saw there was no telephone there. The man had only acted a lie. The officers here gave her no trouble at all and all the threats the first man made were only tricks he had used to try to seduce her.

It was exactly 6:00 p.m. when they drove up to the Pakistani border. The border was closed for the night. There was no one to process their papers. It looked like she would have to spend the night in "no-man's land," a very dangerous place. It is known as the paradise of smugglers. Peter honked the horn. A soldier came out.

Peter said, "It's impossible for a lady to stay here all night. What should we do?"

The soldier thought for a while, then he said, "You may go into the village, but come back tomorrow morning to check your papers."

Very thankful for his kindness, they drove to the busti where the Christian friends put them up for the night. This time Sigi didn't mind staying there. They had some excitement there that night when police came and searched the busti looking for a young man who had deserted the army. He had run home. They found him there and took him away with them.

The next morning, they returned to the border. It was only a mile from the city of Chaman where they had been staying. Their papers were stamped, and they drove back to Quetta.

WAR BREAKS OUT

By this time, Sigi was exhausted from all her experiences and she wanted to go home as quickly as possible. She decided to fly to Kabul rather than endure another long train ride and border-crossing experience. She definitely didn't want to cross the Chaman border into Afghanistan one more time.

Counting her money, she found she had enough to buy an air ticket and still leave a little with Sister Verma. She would not need much, she figured, because she would fly from Quetta to Lahore, transfer immediately on a flight to Kabul, and the following day take her flight to Germany. She had her return ticket from Kabul to Germany. The country was in a state of tension, and if she wanted to get out before war started, she had to go immediately.

It was with a heavy heart Christiana drove her to the airport. She loved Sigi dearly, and it was hard to see her go. She had gone through many trials and lived many years alone. It would be hard to be alone again, especially after the sweet companionship she had had with Sigi.

When they arrived at the airport, Sigi checked her luggage, got her boarding pass, and went through the security check. When she came out, she was able to talk with Christiana, though a fence separated them. She noticed Christiana looked pale and frightened.

"What happened?" asked Sigi.

"The Criminal Investigation Department was just now questioning me. They wanted to know all about you. Who you were, what you were doing here in Quetta, and where you are going. I hope I don't get in trouble after you leave," she whispered. "Maybe they noticed that we visited the chief of the Marri tribe," she added anxiously.

It was true, she and Sigi had visited the chief's home, but only because they had gone to see his wife, a dear friend of Christiana's who had been raised in a Christian school and mission.

Christiana had suffered earlier in 1965, because of her friendship with this family. She had been unexpectedly arrested and imprisoned under a false charge. At that time she was told by the authorities that if she would make a certain statement against the chief, she would be released. They wanted her to say she had seen the chief give a pack of important papers to the Afghans.

This was not true, and she knew they were only trying to bring a false charge against an innocent man in order to incriminate him. She refused to testify falsely against him. They threatened she would never come out of jail but would have to stay there until she died unless she complied. She said then she would stay and die because she was a Christian and could not lie.

She began to fast. When they saw she was not eating, they got worried. The weather was cold. She was given dirty, stinking rags to cover herself but she refused to lie down on the wooden board which served as a bed. She sat up day and night and prayed.

At last they got frightened and released her.

It was no wonder she was afraid again. In these lands, the innocent suffer as much as the guilty, and often more. Sigi prayed with her, committing her to God, and boarded the plane to Lahore on her way to Kabul and Frankfurt.

When she arrived in Lahore, she was informed that the plane for Kabul had just left. She had missed it. She would have to stay overnight to catch the next flight out to Kabul.

She stood helpless, not knowing what to do or where to go. An airlines officer, seeing her standing there looking lost and helpless, walked up to her and said, "I will book you on tomorrow's flight. Meanwhile, you will have to spend the night in Lahore."

Sigi was not expecting to stay in a hotel en route. She had not allowed any money for such expenses. Now she feared there would be not enough for a hotel room. She opened her purse and counted what she had. Yes, thank God, if the room wasn't too expensive, she could manage it for one night. She relaxed. It was good that she didn't know what difficulties were still facing her.

The airlines man was going into the city, so he drove her to a hotel and spoke to the receptionist, asking him to give her a concession, explaining how she had missed her flight. So she got it more cheaply.

It was quite a nice hotel, new and clean, and she was tired, so she settled down for the night.

"I'll write a letter," she thought, "to make use of my time."

Getting out the paper, she sat down at the small writing desk and began writing. Suddenly a great and heavy burden to pray came over her. She was filled with a strange sense of something dreadful about to happen. There was terrible depression. She began to feel like a bird in a cage. The feeling intensified. The very atmosphere was filled with war.

Suddenly the lights went out. She sat stunned. It was pitch dark. She got up and looked out the window. All the lights of the city were out. She stared into the darkness wondering what had happened.

A servant came running to her room. "It is curfew," he shouted. Heavy dark paper was pulled down over the window in her room.

On her table was a small candle. She was permitted to light it. She didn't know what had happened, but she felt that war had broken out. The burden became more intense. Tears were pouring down her cheeks. It seemed the burden was almost more than she could bare. She paced back and forth in her room, praying, trying to quiet her innermost being.

There was a knock on the door. Opening it, she saw the airlines man who had earlier left her here. He was out of breath.

"The war broke out. The war broke out," he gasped. "All flights are cancelled."

This was the worst thing that could happen to her now. She stepped out on the balcony. Lahore was only ten minutes by air from the Indian border. The sirens were wailing continuously. Below on the street, cars were rushing madly, completely in the dark. Again and again she could hear the sound of grinding steel and shattering glass as they collided together in the darkness. The air was filled with the shouts and cries of frightened people. In the distance she saw the firing at the front lines. Now and then the whole place was lighted up with flak. It was hard to tell which was most frightening, the darkness, or the flak lighting which made one feel like he was seen by every evil eye and that there was no hiding place.

She went downstairs to see what was happening. Everyone was very excited. They were gathered around the radio. They expected to hear the announcer tell the good news of great Pakistani victories, for they were sure that Pakistan would win. There was no other way. Every time a Pakistani plane flew over the city, they shouted for joy and pride.

Sigi went back to her room alone. What would she do now? How could she get out of Pakistan? In her heart was the strong impression she must soon get back to Germany. She knew her loved ones, and I, would be anxious and there was no way she could contact us.

And indeed we were very anxious. As soon as I heard the news in Chicago, I became very worried for Sigi's welfare. I didn't have any idea where she was. The last I heard, she was in Quetta, still waiting to get the car fixed. Many began to pray for Sigi's safety from that hour.

Sigi, meanwhile, thought, "There's nothing I can do to-night. I might as well go to bed."

She slept a little, but every time the siren sounded, it woke her, and she would look out the window to see what was happening. As it came closer to morning, she could see the street was full of vehicles, carts, cars, rickshaws, bicycles, buses and trucks. Everything was heavily loaded. The great exodus had begun. People were getting out of Lahore as fast as they could.

As the sun came up, they were afraid their cars would be seen from the air because of the reflection on the windows. In fear, they smeared the windows of their cars so heavily with mud that they could hardly see to drive.

Sigi felt so alone, standing there on the balcony by herself. It seemed everyone had a way out but herself. She began to pray. She started to feel better.

"Ah well!" she finally encouraged herself. "The Lord will make a way for me in spite of the fact I have not much money."

She decided to phone the German Embassy but it was still too early. So she went back to bed and started to doze again. The next thing she knew it was time to phone. When she got the Consulate on the phone she asked the German represen-tative what the condition was, and if any arrangements had been made to get German nationals out of the country.

His reply was far from encouraging. "We have no way of helping you. You'll have to find a way out by yourself. The only way would be overland, across Pakistan to Kabul, and it is getting more dangerous every minute that you stay here. If they blow up the bridges, you will never be able to get out of Lahore. You'd better hurry and leave as quickly as possible."

That was it! She hung up the receiver.

Now she needed a visa for Afghanistan, for the rules are such, that if you go by air, you get it at the airport upon landing, but if you go by land, you need to have it when you cross the border. She looked in the telephone book for the Afghanistan Consulate. It wasn't listed. Upon calling information, she found out that there was none in Lahore. It was situated in Islamabad, the capital.

Islamabad is about four hours drive by car from Lahore. How could she get there? She paced back and forth in her room praying, "God, You have to answer . . . God, You have to answer . . . " and getting more confused and frustrated by the minute.

Then God spoke to her, "I cannot lead you until you have peace in your soul. You cannot hear My voice when you are in a panic. Get still before Me."

She knew this was her answer. She had to get peace in her soul. She got down on her knees and didn't get up until she had it. She was a new Sigi when she stood up and went down to the dining room and ordered breakfast.

At the table near her were seated several German businessmen. They did not know she could understand them. In front of them, on the table, lay their airlines tickets. They were talking about going to the airport to fly somewhere. She was surprised. Hadn't they heard yet what was going on? She wondered.

Just then, another German man walked in. He shouted to these men, "It is true. There are absolutely no flights."

They cursed with anger and were very upset.

Sigi smiled to herself thinking, "Praise God for the peace of God which He can give us in a time of war."

Slowly she walked upstairs, still not knowing what to do. One thing was certain; it was impossible for her to stay there any longer. She had to keep moving. She packed her suitcase and went downstairs to check out. While paying her bill, still wondering what to do and where to go, a man walked up to her and asked her where she was going.

"I have to go to Islamabad to get a visa," she answered.

"We must get there also," he answered. "The only way to do so is to rent a car. Would you be interested in going with us and sharing the expenses? If you would do that, we would gladly take you along."

Hesitatingly, she answered, "What would it cost?"

"The car will cost 400 rupees. If you give one hundred, we will be satisfied." He told her that they were two Polish men working for the government. She wondered if she could afford it. She knew she had to be careful with the little bit of money she had.

As they saw she was still hesitant, he warned her, "You can't go out alone by bus, it is too dangerous for a woman, and on top of it, who knows if the bus could get through?"

She agreed to go along. Together with them, she went to the Intercontinental Hotel where they rented a car and started for Islamabad.

The city was full of excitement. People were wildly running back and forth. War tanks rolled through the streets on their way to the front lines. Sand bags were piled up on the streets. Soldiers were standing at every corner, the bridges were especially heavily guarded. To get out of Lahore, she had to cross these bridges. The air was full of tension.

As they came to the last bridge which leads out of Lahore, she saw a long line waiting to get across the bridge. Cars, trucks, donkeys, and camels were standing, all unattended. They pushed their way into the middle of the bridge, passing the standing, waiting line of traffic. Their driver wanted to stop also but one of the Polish men was shouting at him, "Go! Go! Go!"

Sigi wondered at first what had stopped the traffic from

getting across the bridge. Then she saw Indian war planes overhead. One was flying down low over the bridge strafing it with machine-gun fire. Apparently they had already hit two big electrical power towers which were lying in ruins beside the bridge.

Everyone was afraid to be on the bridge, so they had gotten out of their vehicles, left their animals, and run into the bushes to hide.

The driver wanted to stop the car and get out and run too, but with the Polish man shouting down the back of his neck, he didn't know whether he was more afraid of the Indian war planes or this mad foreigner at his back. He drove like mad between the camels and donkeys and vehicles and they finally crossed safely to the other side. They went so fast, Sigi never had time to see if anyone had been hurt.

Everywhere the roads were jammed with people fleeing. Buses were packed, fully loaded high with everything imaginable. Everyone was trying to get as far away as possible from the border area.

As they drove through towns and villages, they saw masses of people standing by the side of the road. They had garlands in their hands, and as the army went by, they gave them garlands and shouted slogans of victory to encourage them. Sometimes these same people shook their fists at these three foreigners and shouted and cursed at them.

In all the excitement, Sigi had completely forgotten what day of the week it was. "You know it is Saturday, and you won't be able to get a visa until Monday," said one of the men.

Sigi could have groaned. To make it worse, he added, "There is only one decent hotel in Islamabad and that is the Sheraton. If you want a cheaper one, you have to go to Rawalpindi, but you can only reach the embassy by taxi, and that is a long way from there."

While travelling, Sigi thought about it. She said to herself, "I know Gwen gets visas when it's impossible. If she can do it, so can I. I will stay in that expensive hotel one night. God will surely do something for me."

About 4:00 p.m. they arrived in Islamabad. Sigi had a nice room, but she certainly didn't get any enjoyment out of it. This was not the time to relax and look at four pretty walls. She immediately phoned the Afghanistan embassy and explained her problem to the man.

"I'm sorry," he said. "It's impossible for you to get a visa. The embassy is closed till Monday morning. You come then, we will give it to you."

"But," she pleaded, "I must have one today."

"Impossible," he said, and hung up.

She felt sick. "What will I do now?" she cried.

Desperation filled her heart, and she began to cry. "But what is the use of crying? That isn't helping me at all," she said to herself. She remembered the story of the woman in the Bible who was heard because of her much pleading. She decided to phone the man again.

This time he said, "Phone back at 6:00 p.m." Feeling much relieved, she lay down and relaxed. Exactly at six o'clock she phoned the third time.

The man said, "Go to the embassy. There is probably someone there now, but don't tell them that I sent you. Ask him to help you."

Immediately she hurried downstairs to call a taxi. When she reached the lobby, the sirens began to wail. It was impossible to go.

Dejected, she turned and went back to her room to wait. Looking out the window she could see that the darkened sky was lit up like a red fire – a plane dogfight.

Over the hotel public address system, the latest news told of big victories Pakistan was having over India on every front. Everyone was excited. They were sure of victory. Sigi's heart felt heavy and sad for she felt that the people were not being told the truth, and that before it was all over, Pakistan would suffer great and terrible tragedies.

Finally, about two-and-a-half hours later, the all-clear siren sounded. Again she went downstairs.

"Can I go outside?" she asked the receptionist.

"Yes," he answered.

"Get me a taxi, please."

"No, I can't do that. It's too dangerous. It's still blackout. It is almost impossible to drive in the dark without lights." It was December when the days are very short. The sun went down early and it began to get dark at about 5:30 p.m. By then it was pitch dark.

"But I have to go to the embassy," she said.

"Well, if you insist, I'll get you a taxi," he said, "but it will be at your own risk."

"That's okay," she answered gladly.

Never in her life would she forget that ride. Not only was it completely dark, but the taxi was completely covered with mud. The mud was used as camouflage. Even the windows were so covered it was almost impossible to see out of them in daytime, let alone in the night.

The driver got in and started the car. The embassy was only about four miles away, but it seemed to take a lifetime to get there. He drove in the darkness as fast as he could drive. Sigi tried to look out but it was impossible to see a thing. She sat back and prayed. Suddenly they came to an abrupt stop. They had almost hit a camel.

Again, they started out. Again he slammed on the brakes and she flew out of her seat. This time he had almost hit a car. In his hurry he missed the turn but luckily found his way back and stopped in front of the embassy. She staggered up to the door and rang the bell.

An old watchman came out and told her to wait awhile. She waited on the doorstep till he returned with a candle and led her into the dark building. She found herself in the kitchen. Another man was there. He seemed to have authority.

She told him her story. To her great relief, she found him to be both friendly and understanding. He gave her the visa immediately, right there in the kitchen, by candlelight! With God all things ARE possible. She smiled to herself, and walked out the door with a thankful heart.

"I have the same wonderful God that Gwen has," she thought.

Her taxi was waiting when she came out. The drive back to the hotel was no less hazardous than the first one. Once they almost hit some people who were walking on the street.

When she stepped into the hotel, she had time to look about and see for the first time what was going on. In the dimness of the candle light, she saw the place was full of businessmen, most of whom were waiting for a flight out of Pakistan.

"They will wait a long time," thought Sigi, as she watched them.

There was a big businessman there from Italy. He was going to Indonesia. He told Sigi how bored he was with waiting and waiting. "There's nothing to do but wait," he complained.

She told him she was leaving the next day by bus for Peshawar and the Afghanistan border. He was aghast.

"What will happen to you? Aren't you afraid? The roads might close up, and you are alone."

"I'm not alone," she answered.

"But," he said, with a big question on his face, "you just said you are alone."

"I'm alone, and I'm NOT alone," she replied smugly.

Now he was really confused. So she told him about her Friend, Jesus Christ. He looked at her as if she were telling him a big fairy tale and shook his head. Never in his life had he heard anything like that!

At seven o'clock the next morning, Sigi came downstairs to pay her bill. The man looked at her in surprise.

"Where do you think you are going?" he asked.

"I am leaving."

"No, you can't do that. Nobody leaves. Everyone stays here. The roads are closed. You can't get through," he warned.

"I have to leave anyway," she answered. "I must take that

chance."

Seeing her determination, he ordered a taxi.

She had gone about two miles when the siren sounded. A policeman stood in the middle of the road stopping all traffic. He ordered them to drive the car to the side of the road and park it in the bushes where all the cars were already standing. He ordered every car that came along to do the same thing.

"Oh no," thought Sigi. "I will miss my bus."

It was supposed to leave in a few minutes for Peshawar. She prayed, "Lord, make that driver go. You know I have to catch the bus."

Just then, the policeman turned his back to them. The driver pulled out onto the street and drove like mad (about 70 kilometers per hour!) and didn't stop till he reached the bus station.

There was a great crowd at the bus station. It seemed like everyone in the city was trying to catch a bus. It was impossible to move. Again fear entered her heart that she might not be able to get a bus. She was still in the taxi. The driver finally got upset with the crowd and, pushing them out of the way, drove her up to where the bus was standing ready to leave.

It was a mini-bus. She climbed inside and found a seat, and in a minute, was on her way. She had just made it in time!

It was quite a pleasant and uneventful journey. All along the way, Sigi could see tanks, soldiers, and trucks hidden in the bushes. As they neared Peshawar, she saw a big high bridge. It was over the Indus River. There was a big sign which read, "Taking photos is forbidden."

As they drove up, she noticed two men were being held by the police. Later on, she was to meet them accidently. They told how they had stopped to take a look and their film was confiscated by the police even though they had not taken any pictures. Everyone was very nervous.

It was 11:00 a.m. when they arrived in Peshawar. Immediately she inquired what time the bus left for Kabul. The first one would be the next morning at seven o'clock. So she had to spend the night there.

Since the bus ticket was quite inexpensive, she immediately bought it for the next day. This left her with about eight dollars. Now she had to find a room for the night.

The best, she thought, would be to stay in the one across from the bus station. But the Lord stopped her; He said, "Go back to the Dennis Hotel!"

"But Lord, that's where that man was who gave me all that trouble. I certainly don't want to go there!" Sigi complained.

However, she felt a strong urge that she just had to go there. She stopped a motor rickshaw, jumped in, and started out with a very reluctant feeling.

As soon as she arrived, the first thing she did was to look around and see if that man were there. But she couldn't see him anywhere. Relieved, she booked her room, took a bath, and went out to sit on the lawn.

She saw that the place was literally filled with foreign men. There must have been about 30 or 40 of them. They were all speaking German.

She thought, "I'm going to sit here until someone talks to me, and it won't take long."

Sure enough! In a little while, someone spoke to her. As soon as he found out she was a German, he said, "Why don't you come along with us? We have been working here with a certain German company and are all leaving together. We have been here since morning waiting for the Afghanistan authorities to give us our visas. As soon as we are ready, we are going in cars to the border. Now you might as well come along with us. No one would know the difference."

Sigi was thrilled at the idea. She would be able to get across to Kabul one day earlier, and that much easier.

At 4:30 they got the papers they were waiting for. Sigi ran upstairs to pack. On her way she met the manager. He remembered her from the time before and was surprised to see her. When she explained what had happened and that she had to leave, he kindly gave her the money back which she had paid for her room. She was thankful for it. Later she direly needed it.

About 5:00 p.m. they started out for the border. Usually the border closed at 6:00 p.m., but the German embassy had arranged with the authorities to keep the border open until 11:00 p.m. that day in order to permit all these Germans to get across. The German consul himself was at the border and made sure everything went smoothly. Never had she seen such a large group of people cross over a border in this part of the world so quickly before.

It was very late and the roads were dangerous, so when they reached Jalalabad, they spent the night in a hotel. Sigi was glad she had gotten her money back from the last hotel. She needed it now.

The next day, about noon, they all arrived in Kabul. Sigi went to her friends, the Johnsons, and spent the night with them. She wanted to send me a telegram, but she didn't have enough money.

The following day, December 7, 1971, she flew to Germany. In her purse she had one dollar and one German mark (about 33 cents).

Part Five

The India-Pakistan war of 1971 had been building up for a long time. Tension was continually increasing. On November 7, Mr. Z.A. Bhutto, the prime minister of Pakistan, had warned that if war broke out between India and Pakistan, it would be a total war, "a house-to-house conflict." He further stated that the waters of the Ganges (in India) and the Indus (in Pakistan) would flow red as a result of the bloodshed.

On the 22nd of November, Pakistani Sabre jets which intruded into Indian air space were shot down near Calcutta. Two of the pilots bailed out and were captured. Again the Pakistan International Airlines cancelled all domestic flights into Dacca leaving it cut off from the rest of Bangladesh.

On the 23rd, Pakistan declared a state of emergency.

On the 24th, curfew was again clamped on Dacca. The situation was tense. Things continued much the same until the end of the month.

On December 1, United States suspended licensing of arms shipments to India.

On December 2, the day before war began, Prime Minister Indira Gandhi warned, "Peace can return to the subcontinent only if the Pakistani army withdraws from the borders of India, in the west, as well as in the east."

On December 3, around 5:40 p.m., the Pakistan Air Force attacked 12 targets in India. They were airfields and defensive positions all along the western sector.

There was an immediate counterattack by Indian air and ground forces in both the east and the west. Emergency was proclaimed in India.

Early on the morning of December 4, Indian ground forces started moving into East Pakistan (Bangladesh), joining up with the freedom fighters who had been carrying on guerilla warfare during the past nine months. The strategy of the

Indian forces was to bypass the main cities in order to avoid large civilian casualties and prevent damage to national assets. This strategy surprised war experts around the world.

Within the first 24 hours the Indian Air Force completely destroyed the few Pakistani Air Force planes which had been left in Bangladesh.

Paratroopers, dropped by helicopters in the rear, joined the other fighting forces.

The Indian Air Force under the command of Marshal P.C. Lal, the Navy under the command of Admiral S.M. Nanda, and the Army under the command of Field Marshal Manekshaw worked together in perfect unity. The Navy immobilized the ports in Chittagong and in the Khellna-Cholna Mongla complex, and Cox's Bazaar, cutting off all escape routes in Bangladesh.

Although the Pakistani troops fought bravely, their commanders did not pay heed to the messages of Gen. Manekshaw of India to save their lives. India pleaded with the W. Pakistan commanders to surrender in order to save the lives of their men.

On December 8, this message was sent: "From General Manekshaw, Chief of the Army Staff of India, to the Pakistan armed forces at present attempting to collect and concentrate at Narayanganj and Barisal:

' I know you are concentrating in these areas in the hope that you will be able to escape or be picked up. I have taken measures to prevent you from getting away by sea and have deployed Naval forces appropriately. Should you not heed my advice to surrender to my Army and endeavour to escape, I assure you a certain fate awaits you. Do not say that I have not warned you. Once you surrender, you shall be treated with dignity as per the Geneva Convention."

But even if they felt inclined to do so, the commanders were overruled by the Pakistani leaders who were issuing orders out of West Pakistan.

Day after day, the West Pakistani army in Bangladesh was falling back and India was gaining more ground, until within a week, half of the Pakistani Occupation Army was encircled by the combined forces of the Freedom Fighters and the Indian Army.

On December 13, the United States ordered its Seventh Fleet, headed by the nuclear aircraft carrier Enterprise, to move into the Bay of Bengal. This aroused the suspicions of India, and created an anti-American wave throughout India which prevails to this day.

The U.S.S.R. accused the U.S.A. of attempts to blackmail India by sending its Seventh Fleet to the Bay of Bengal. Meanwhile, a powerful Soviet Naval fleet was reported to be moving into the Bay of Bengal.

On December 14, Malik, the West Pakistani governor in Dacca, resigned and sought sanctuary in a neutral zone under the protection of the Red Cross.

Meanwhile, on the western front, the fight to protect Indian soil against Pakistan's furious onslaught was fierce. Indian soldiers stood their ground with determination and thrust the Pakistani troops back to their own territory, and in so doing, carried the war deep into Pakistan. The famous city of Sialkot was virtually under seige. It would have fallen if the cease-fire had been put off another 12 hours.

The Indian Air Force struck by day and by night without interruption at the aircraft on the ground, the airfield installations, and the radar stations. Troop concentrations were broken up and armed columns were scattered. West Pakistani Aircraft which ventured into India suffered heavy tolls.

The Naval Command of India successfully held back the Pakistani fleet, and prevented it from striking Indian ports. Two daring attacks were launched by India at Karachi and were successful in damaging port and shore installations. Great oil and fuel tanks were blown up lighting the skies of Karachi for days and making the port city a well-lit target for Indian air attacks by day and by night.

With Dacca completely surrounded on the east and the Indian forces gaining ground in the west, Pakistan learned she was fighting a losing war. Still it is hard to give up when one has been so confident of success. The lives of tens of thousands of soldiers were hanging in the balance. These were the brave Pathans, the great warriors of West Pakistan, who now were more or less captives in the city of Dacca. The order had come from the West Pakistani government that they must fight till the last man.

The Indian Commander, Gen. Manekshaw, sent a final warning on December 13 to Major General Farman Ali, commander of the garrison at Dacca. In this warning he said: "I have appealed to you twice already. But there has been no response from you so far. I wish to repeat that further resistance is senseless and will mean death to many poor soldiers under your command quite unnecessarily. . . . My forces are now closing in around Dacca and your garrisons there are within the range of my artillery. I have issued instructions to my troops to afford complete protection to foreign nationals and all ethnic minorities (civilians who do not hail from Bangladesh itself). It should be the duty of all commanders to prevent useless shedding of innocent blood, and I am therefore appealing to you once again to cooperate with me in discharging this humane responsibility. . . . Should you, however, decide to continue to offer resistance, may I strongly urge that you ensure that all civilians and foreign nationals are removed to safe distance from the area of conflict. For the sake of your own men, I hope you will not compel me to reduce your garrison by the use of force."

All the world looked on in anxiety. In Chicago I prayed with great concern. I still remember late that night, with the world waiting for the troops in Dacca to surrender, knowing that if they did not, millions would die and the streets would flow with the blood of multitudes of innocent. It seemed as if my spirit left my body and I was lifted above the city of Dacca. There I saw the two great armies amassed, and feeling only love in my heart for both the Pakistanis and the Indians, I wept, that precious lives might be spared and that their commander in charge would surrender to the Indian army which had them surrounded.

The events preceding the surrender were interesting and dramatic.

December 15th, Gen. Miasi had sent a cease-fire offer with the concurrence of Yahya Khan, but he failed to respond to the final warning of the Indian Chief of Army Staff, Gen. Manekshaw, for unconditional surrender, till 8:00 a.m. on December 16th, only half an hour before the time limit given to him for making a decision.

The Indian army was preparing to wipe out the besieged defenders of Dacca when they received a request for an extension of six hours. At the same time they requested that an Indian Army Staff Officer be sent to negotiate terms of surrender. Gen. Manekshaw granted this extension. As a measure of generosity, he offered strict adherence to the Geneva Convention even to the commander of an army which had butchered between 1.5 and 2 million people during the last nine months.

At 10:40 a.m. the Instrument of Surrender was handed over. The Indian army had at that time entered Dacca without any opposition.

At 2:45 p.m. it was accepted.

At 3:30 p.m. Maj. Gen. Ansarj of the Pakistan Division laid down his arms before Maj. Gen. Brar of the Indian Army.

At 4:31 p.m. the Instrument of Surrender was formally signed in Dacca by Lt. Gen. Niasi.

After signing the Instrument of Surrender, Gen. Niasi stripped off his epaulet of rank from his right shoulder, unloaded his revolver, handed over the bullets to Gen. Aurora, and finally pressed his forehead to that of Gen. Aurora as an act of humble submission and surrender. It was a moment of utter humiliation for the Pakistani general, and soon after the ritual of signing, there was a volley of abuses and insults from the Bengali crowd which had assembled there to witness the end of the drama and the end of the military rule of Pakistan in their land.

India permitted the thousands of Pakistani soldiers to keep their guns as they marched into the cantonment where they were imprisoned until they could be sent into India. This gesture of goodwill was the thing which saved their lives, for had they not been able to protect themselves, the angry masses of Dacca who had suffered under their cruelty for nine months would have turned on these men and torn them to pieces like wild animals.

The story was told to us that when the crowds which surrounded these marching men shouted, "Jai Bangla!" (Victory for Bengali!) the soldiers would shoot into the crowd killing the ones who had dared to voice their joy at the defeat of Pakistan.

But still the joy could not be crushed. Thousands in Dacca danced and cheered and wept for joy as Lt. Gen. Sagat Singh led the first column of victorious Indian troops and Freedom Fighters into the Bangladesh capital of Dacca.

That same day, Prime Minister Indira Ghandi ordered unilateral cease-fire on the western front to be effective the following day, December 17, at 8:00 p.m., and urged Pakistan to accept it.

Twenty-four hours later, Radio Pakistan announced Yahya Khan's acceptance of India's offer.

And so it was, that 14 days after the war had begun, it had ended. Asia would never be the same again. The map would now show a new nation: Bangladesh.

Indian war records read like a storybook fantasy:

Indian Air Force bombers and fighters had carried out 4,000 sorties on West Pakistan.

Indian Air Force had destroyed 72 or more aircraft, 156 tanks, 76 goods trains, two warships, two submarines, 16 gunboats, two mine-sweepers.

Indian Air Force smashed three oil refineries.

And 93,000 Prisoners[7] of War from Pakistan were in captivity while 617 Indian soldiers were in Pakistan captivity.

Part Six

On January 21, 1973, at 12 noon, Sigi and I landed at Dacca airport, Bangladesh. It was a great thrill for us. We had watched the birth of this nation with anxious eyes, and in our small way, mostly only by our prayers, had had a part in its beginning.

The first thing which impressed us was its poverty. Even 13 months after its beginning, it was struggling for existence. Everywhere one could feel the tension of fear: fear of violence, fear of treachery, fear of hunger, fear of the darkness, fear of what tomorrow would bring.

The two leading hotels in the city were crowded to capacity with foreigners who had come to Bangladesh to assist in relief programs, traders, and other government servants. It was like a small United Nations. They were there from all over the world.

An attempt had been made on the life of their Prime Minister Sheik Mujibur Rehman. Bangabandhu (Father of the Nation), as he is affectionately called by his people, had suffered with his people and for them. For over ten years of his life he had been in jails. Yet, every time he was released, he bravely stood for the truth and risked his life to give his people independence.

When he was arrested in the early hours of March 26, 1971, and secretly taken to West Pakistan, the world was anxious for him. That same night President Yahya Khan had announced on Radio Pakistan that Rehman was "an enemy of Pakistan and his crime would not go unpunished."

A great wave of anger swept the world and almost all governments urged Yahya Khan not to harm Rehman whose only crime was his love for the people. Yet, in spite of public opinion, Khan put him on trial on August 11th.

After cease-fire, he was released on January 8, by President

Bhutto and flown to London by an R.A.F. plane of the British government.

From there he was flown to Dacca by way of Delhi where he made a three-hour stopover. In a public meeting, he thanked the people of India for their support in the liberation of Bangladesh.

The same afternoon, January 9th, he arrived in Dacca where ten million people were at the airport to welcome him. Dacca rejoiced to have their beloved "Bangabandhu" home.

He told his nation how for nine months he had been kept in ignorance of what was going on in Bangladesh. Now the sudden shock of hearing about the atrocities broke his heart. It was almost more than he could bear. And yet he could say, "I have nothing against West Pakistan, in spite of the way they have behaved. When they arrested me, they arrested my children, too, and interned them, and my house was burned. I am shocked to know how millions of my people have been killed and tortured mercilessly. Even if Hitler were alive, he would have been ashamed. We are still calculating, and the final figure of those killed may be over three million.

"Daughters were raped in front of their fathers and mothers, and women were raped in front of their husbands and sons. I cannot stop my tears when I think of it.

"I am grateful to the freedom-loving people all over the world, including the U.S.A., who supported us in our struggle for freedom."

He told of the trial at which he was condemned to be hanged, and said, "I was mentally ready to die. The day I went to jail, I didn't know whether I was to live or die. But I knew that Bangladesh would be liberated."

Now, one year later, he again stood before his people in the same great Dacca Race Course and told them, "If the people of Bangladesh don't want me to contest the elections, then I don't want to sit in the National Assembly. Any one of you can go and sit there instead of me. Shall I contest the election? If you want me to contest, then raise your hand. Raise both your hands to show you want me."

Nearly half a million pairs of skinny brown hands waved in the air shouting, "Yes, yes, yes! We want you Bangabandhu!"

But whether or not he can continue to lead his people, no one knows. Subversive elements in all lands seek to destroy the great and good leaders of today.

After the terrible cyclone and tidal wave of 1970, in which at least half a million people lost their lives, and the drought of 1972, the nation is on the brink of starvation. In spite of 1.2 billion dollars in relief, (32.8 million from the U.S.A. has made her the largest contributor), a government authority told us that two million face starvation in the immediate future.

Everywhere, we felt or saw signs of unrest. At night men walking in groups of a hundred, armed with clubs, marched the streets. By day, people gathered in groups attracted by a man swallowing fire just outside the gates of the place where we stayed. When he got the crowd together, he spoke to them for two-and-a-half hours. I timed him. He was stirring them up to make demands and expect conditions which a poverty-stricken government cannot give.

One after the other told us stories of how their loved ones had been killed. Others told how whole villages had been wiped out by fires purposely set by the Pakistani soldiers. Many young girls who had been kept by the West Pakistani soldiers had committed suicide. Others had given their babies away for adoption. Some kept their babies, for in spite of the horror of the circumstances of their conception (rape), they still loved their own flesh and blood. A few had gone through the ordeal of abortions.

Prime Minister Rehman had pleaded with the young men who had been Freedom Fighters to come forward and offer to marry these girls, saying they could not help what had happened to them, that they were the victims of the cruelties of war. According to strict Muslim rules, the men would have nothing to do with them. But as a result of his appeal, one young man took the first of these girls as his bride the week we were there and they were honoured with gifts by the

Prime Minister and his wife.

As we stood to speak before the dear people I felt so unworthy. Who was I? What could I say to people who suffered such untold agonies?

The faces were full of suffering and some had bitter memories. The name of Pakistan was never to be spoken audibly in Bangladesh.

"Oh God, what can I say to them?" I prayed.

And then I heard again the words of our Lord: "Love your enemies, bless them that curse you, do good to them that hate you, and pray for them that despitefully use you . . . that ye may be the children of your Father which is in heaven."

It is not enough to be a citizen of a nation, not even Bangladesh. It is important one makes sure he is a citizen of heaven and a child of God. To be a member of an earthly kingdom is easy – one can hate and curse and be cruel. But to belong to God's kingdom, one must have love, one must forgive.

Bangladesh needs to love all, even her own enemies! For only then will she be healed. She needs to forgive, for then she will do the works of God. And only then can she become great.

And who is Bangladesh? Not the fields and hills and rivers, but every beautiful brown-eyed man, woman, and child who has suffered and lived through nine months of agony and travail.

Yes, she has been born a nation, and has her place in the nations of the world. Now it remains for her wound to be healed, her tears to be dried, and her heart filled with love and forgiveness so that she can say with her leader, the great father of the nation, the beloved Bangabandhu, "I have nothing against the people of West Pakistan."

Only a great man can speak like that.

Such a great man was the One who hung bloody on the cross, and looking down at His enemies prayed, "Father, forgive them, for they know not what they do."

So great is the love and forgiveness of God that few humans can begin to fathom its depths. God loves and forgives the man no matter how vile the deed. God's grace and mercy is today extended to the 93,000 Pakistan prisoners of war as surely as it was to the victims of their atrocities. He even loves the generals and the high-ranking officers who were responsible for the death of multitudes.

Out of West Pakistan comes this beautiful and true story which is a proof of this great love of God.

Among the West Pakistani soldiers stationed in Bangladesh was a man, Captain Yousif. He was engaged in fighting, carrying out the orders of his commanding officers, killing men, women, and children. He was as bad as the rest of them. While engaged in war, he was wounded.

After being wounded, he was sent back to Rawalpindi in West Pakistan where he was admitted to the military hospital. While he was there, it developed that he had severe heart trouble. Because they did not have the necessary facilities to take care of him, he was transferred to the Roman Catholic Hospital in Rawalpindi for special treatment for his heart.

Instead of improving, he got worse, and one day he had a massive heart attack and died.

The hospital staff gathered around and tried to revive him but they were unable to do anything to help him. He was pronounced dead.

When he died, he experienced his spirit leaving his body. He was very much aware that he had come outside and was in a country area. The sun was shining brightly. He saw an old man under a tree. Near the old man was a flock of sheep. Captain Yousif gathered that this old man was the shepherd. He went over and sat down beside him.

The old man turned to him and said, "Jesus is coming to see you."

Captain Yousif was a Muslim. He did not know who Jesus was because in his language, in the language of their Koran, His name is pronounced differently.

Shortly thereafter, he left the old man and went on. Suddenly a bright light shone in front of him. He was dazzled by its brilliance and wondered what it meant. Then he saw a beautiful man step out from that light and come to him. He wondered who this person was.

Suddenly the person spoke and said, "I am Jesus!"

Captain Yousif saw that there were wounds on His head, and blood was running down. He showed him the nail scars in His hands and feet and side.

The Lord Jesus spoke again and said, "I will not let you die."

Then He took His own finger, dipped it in the blood from His forehead and reaching over, made the sign of the cross with it on Captain Yousif's chest, right over his heart.

"I have work for you to do," Jesus said to him.

The next thing he knew, the captain was re-entering his body in the hospital.

He opened his eyes and looked around. A nurse saw him and anxiously asked, "Are you all right?"

"Yes," he said, "but who is Jesus? Tell me, who is Jesus?"

She apparently didn't know.

"Get someone to tell me," he begged.

Another nurse, standing nearby, heard him and said, "I'm a follower of Jesus. I'll tell you who He is."

He listened in wonder as the beautiful story of Jesus, His love, and His death was told to him. Then he told the nurse what had happened to him.

The hospital staff in charge of him was called back to see him. They were amazed when they saw he was alive. Upon examining him, they discovered that he had been healed. His wounds were all healed up and his heart was normal.

He was told that he could go home.

When he started to dress, he noticed blood on his chest. Then he remembered that this was where Jesus had touched him.

When he returned home and witnessed to his very strict Muslim father, it created a great ruckus. His father became angry and told him to get out of the house. He went to live with a friend.

A few days later a friend warned him that his father was planning to shoot him.

"I am not worrying," he said. "Jesus told me I wouldn't die. I have a work to do for Him."

Today Captain Yousif is witnessing for Christ throughout West Pakistan.

How marvelous it is that God should choose a man like this to bear witness for Him of His love and mercy! God had forgiven him because He loves him.

Only this kind of love can give us the strength to forgive our enemies.

THE END

THE LAST CALL

Again a second time into this world you cannot come,
So take each opportunity to do good deeds today;
For any good that you may do, or love that you may give,
If now delayed, will ne'er be done – for time flees fast away.

Time flies as quickly as the bird that soars high on the wind,
And like the river, flows down hill, cannot return again.
It's like the body of a one, beloved, now cold in death;
A thousand tears, a thousand calls, can't waken her again.

Your life on earth, this gift of God, few treasure as they
should,
It passes much too suddenly, and never more returns.
Now do thy best, before the slap of death has stilled thy
voice,
And if you want to pray, pray now; yea, all good virtues
learn.

And when you stand by someone's grave, and bid farewell
with tears,
Let it remind you, pilgrim dear, someday you'll leave here,
too.
You're not a child who must be taught life's greatest truths
by force;
You're old enough to see and know, and to yourself be true.

Abdurrahman (called Rahman Baba)
18th century Pathan poet

More Life-Changing Books

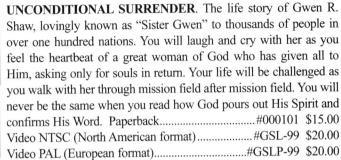

1

IN THE BEGINNING — *A daily devotional based on the book of Genesis.* The Book of Genesis is perhaps the most important book in the Old Testament. It is the foundation stone of all knowledge and wisdom. Deep and wonderful truths hidden in the pages of Genesis are revealed in this devotional book. You'll be amazed at the soul-stirring writings inspired by the well-known stories of Genesis. Hardcover
.... #000211 $27.95

DEEPEN YOUR WALK WITH GOD WITH
CLASSIC ANOINTED BIBLE STUDIES BY GWEN SHAW!

BEHOLD THE BRIDEGROOM COMETH! A Bible study on the soon return of Jesus Christ. With so many false teachings these days, it is important that we realize how imminent the rapture of the saints of God really is...#000304 $6.50

 ENDUED WITH LIGHT TO REIGN FOREVER. This deeply profound Bible study reveals the characteristics of the eternal, supernatural, creative light of God as found in His Word. The "Father of Lights," created man in His image. He longs for man to step out of darkness and into His light..#000306 $5.00

GOD'S END-TIME BATTLE-PLAN. This study on spiritual warfare gives you the biblical weapons for spiritual warfare such as victory through dancing, shouting, praising, uplifted hands, marching, etc. It has been a great help to many who have been bound by tradition. ....#000305 $8.00

 IT'S TIME FOR REVIVAL. A Bible study on revival that not only gives scriptural promises of the end-time revival, but also presents the stories of revivals in the past and the revivalists whom God used. It will stir your heart and encourage you to believe for great revival!
.... #000311 $7.75

OUR MINISTERING ANGELS. A scriptural Bible study on the topic of angels. Angels will be playing a more and more prominent part in these last days. We need to understand about them and their ministry. Read exciting accounts of angelic help.........#000308 $7.50

POUR OUT YOUR HEART. A wonderful Bible study on travailing prayer. The hour has come to intercede before the throne of God. The call to intercession is for everyone, and we must carry the Lord's burden and weep for the lost so that the harvest can be brought in quickly .... #000301 $5.00

REDEEMING THE LAND. A Bible study on spiritual warfare. This important teaching will help you know your authority through the Blood of Jesus to dislodge evil spirits, break the curse, and restore God's blessing upon the land .... #000309 $9.50

THE FINE LINE. This Bible study clearly magnifies the "fine line" of difference between the soul realm and the spirit realm. Both are intangible and therefore cannot be discerned with the five senses, but must be discerned by the Holy Spirit and the Word of God. A must for the deeper Christian..#000307 $6.00

THE POWER OF THE PRECIOUS BLOOD. A Bible study on the Blood of Jesus. The author shares how it was revealed to her how much Satan fears Jesus' Blood. This Bible study will help you overcome and destroy the works of Satan in your life and the lives of loved ones! .... #000303 $5.00

THE POWER OF PRAISE. When God created the heavens and the earth, He was surrounded by praise. Miracles happen when holy people praise a Holy God! Praise is the language of creation. If prayer can move the hand of God, how much more praise can move Him! .... #000312 $5.00

YE SHALL RECEIVE POWER FROM ON HIGH. This is a much needed foundational teaching on the Baptism of the Holy Spirit. It will enable you to teach this subject, as well as to understand these truths more fully yourself...#000310 $5.00

YOUR APPOINTMENT WITH GOD. A Bible study on fasting. Fasting is one of the most neglected sources of power over bondages of Satan that God has given the Church. The author's experiences shared in this Bible study will change your life...........#000302 $5.00

FORGIVE AND RECEIVE. This Bible Study is a lesson to the church on the much-needed truths of forgiveness and restoration. The epistle to Philemon came from the heart of Paul who had experienced great forgiveness ....#000406 $7.00

GRACE ALONE. This study teaches the reader to gain freedom in the finished work of the Cross by forsaking works (which cannot add to salvation) and live by *Grace Alone*............. #000402 $13.00

MYSTERY REVEALED. Search the depths of God's riches in one of Paul's most profound epistles, "to the praise of His glory!" Learn the "mystery" of the united Body of Christ as revealed in the book of Ephesians..#000403 $15.00

OUR GLORIOUS HEAD. This book teaches vital truths for today, assisting the reader in discerning false teachings, when the philosophies of men are being promoted as being the truths of God. Jesus Christ is the Head of His Body!.................... #000404 $9.00

THE CATCHING AWAY! This is a very timely Bible study because Jesus is coming soon! The book of 1 Thessalonians explains God's revelation to Paul on the rapture of the saints. 2 Thessalonians reveals what will happen after the rapture when the antichrist takes over..#000407 $13.00

THE LOVE LETTER. This expository study of the letter to the first church of Europe will give the reader an understanding of Paul's great love for the church that was born out of his suffering. ....#000405 $9.00

POPULAR BIBLE COURSE

THE TRIBES OF ISRAEL. This popular and well-loved study on the thirteen tribes of Israel will show you your place in the spiritual tribes in these last days. Understand yourself and others better through the study of this Bible Course!
.... #000501 $45.00 • Set of 13 tapes #TGS1 $42.00

4

SONG OF LOVE. She was a heart-broken missionary, far from home. She cried out to God for help. He spoke, "Turn to the Song of Solomon and read!" As she turned in obedience, the Lord took her into the "Throne Room" of Heaven and taught her about the love of Christ for His Bride, the church. She fell in love with Jesus afresh, and you will too..#000401 $8.95

 THE FALSE FAST. Now, from the pen of Gwen Shaw, author of Your Appointment With God (a Bible Study on fasting), comes an exposé on the False Fast. It will help you to examine your motives for fasting, and make your foundations sure, so that your fast will be a potent tool in the hands of God ....#000602 $2.50

THE LIGHT WILL COME FROM RUSSIA. The thrilling testimony of Mother Barbara, Abbess of the Mount of Olives in Jerusalem. She shares prophecies which were given to her concerning the nations of the world in our time by a holy bishop of the Kremlin, ten days before his death just prior to the Russian Revolution. Includes a fascinating history of the final days of the royal family.............#000606 $5.50

 THE PARABLE OF THE GOLDEN RAIN. This is the story of how revivals come and go, and a true picture, in parable language, of how the Church tries to replace the genuine move of the Spirit with man-made programs and tactics. It's amusing and convicting at the same time..#000603 $4.00

THEY SHALL MOUNT UP WITH WINGS AS EAGLES. Though you may feel old or tired, if you wait on the Lord, you shall mount up on wings as eagles! Let this book encourage you to stretch your wings and fulfill your destiny — no matter what your age! ....#000604 $6.95

 TO BE LIKE JESUS. Based on her Throne Room experience in 1971, the author shares the Father's heart about our place as sons in His Family. Nothing is more important than To Be Like Jesus! ....#000605 $6.95

POCKET SERMON BOOKS BY GWEN SHAW

BEHOLD, THIS DREAMER COMETH. Dreams and dreamers are God's gift to humanity to bring His purposes into the hearts of mankind. The life of Joseph, the dreamer, will encourage you to believe God to fulfill the dream He has put into your heart ....#000707 $2.00

BREAKTHROUGH. Just like when Peter was in prison, sometimes you need a "breakthrough" in your life! This book reveals the truth in a fresh and living way!...#000708 $2.00

 DON'T STRIKE THE ROCK! When Moses became angry with the people's rebellion and disobeyed God's order to speak to the Rock, it cost him his entrance into the Promised Land. Don't allow anything to keep you from fulfilling God's perfect will for your life!...#000704 $2.00

FROM PEAK TO PEAK. Mountains are the challenges that God puts in our lives and the peaks are places of destiny that He lays before us. Press in to God to find the courage that only He gives to take you from peak to peak to fulfill His destiny for you......... #000718 $2.00

 GOD WILL DESTROY THE VEIL OF BLINDNESS. "...as the veil of the Temple was rent...I shall again rend the veil in two....for... the Arab, so they shall know that I am God...." This was the word of the Lord concerning God's plan for the nations in the days to come. Join in with Abraham's prayer "Let Ishmael live before Thee!"............... #000712 $2.00

HASTENING OUR REDEMPTION. All of Heaven and Earth are waiting for the Body of Christ to rise up in maturity and reclaim what we lost in the Fall of Man. Applying the Blood of Jesus is the key to *Hastening Our Redemption* ....#000705 $2.00

 IT CAN BE AVERTED. Many people today are burdened and fearful over prophecies of doom and destruction. However, the Bible is clear that God prefers mercy over judgment when His people humble themselves and pray...#000706 $2.00

IT'S TIME FOR CHANGE—After 911, everyone has agreed that "Things will never be the same!" But thank God! The Almighty is still on the throne, and nothing can happen that He does not permit! Let Him prepare you for change! ....#000714 $2.00

 KAIROS TIME. That once in a lifetime opportunity—that second, or minute, or hour, or year, or even longer, when a golden opportunity is sovereignly given to us by the Almighty. What we do with it can change our lives and possibly even change the world..................#000709 $2.00

KNOWING ONE ANOTHER IN THE SPIRIT. Find great peace as you learn to understand the difficulties your friends, enemies and loved ones face that help to form their character. "Wherefore henceforth know we no man after the flesh..." (II Cor. 5:16a) ...... #000703 $2.00

7

TEACH THEM TO WEEP. "My people don't know how to pray!" I answered, "How can I teach them to pray?" He said, "It's too late to teach them to pray. But you can teach them to weep." .... #000716 $2.00

 THAT WE MAY BE ONE. Only one thing can unite the children of the Lord: the Glory of God. One of Jesus' last prayers was that all of God's children might be one. His prayer still rings out across the ages and convicts us of our lack of unity! .... #000715 $2.00

THE ANOINTING BREAKS THE YOKE. Learn how the anointing of God can set you free from your bondage: free to fulfill your destiny in the call of God on your life! .... #000710 $2.00

 THE CHANGING OF THE GUARD. This seasoned General in God's army, veteran of many battles of faith, challenges the next generation to take up the torch and "do or die" in following the call of God upon their lives. You will be challenged to give up all for the cause of Christ .... #000719 $2.00

THE CHURCH OF THE OPEN ARMS — *Gwen Shaw.* Sister Gwen had a life-changing dream that has given her a fresh vision for the lost and for loving the unlovely. It is time to answer the call to be "The Church of the Open Arms" .... #000713 $2.00

 THE CRUCIFIED LIFE. When you suffer, knowing the cause is not your own sin, for you have searched your heart before God, then you must accept that it is God doing a new thing in your life. Let joy rise up within you because you are a partaker of Christ's suffering......... #000701 $2.00

THE MASTER IS COME AND CALLETH FOR THEE. Read about how the Lord called Gwen Shaw to begin the ministry of the End-Time Handmaidens and Servants. Perhaps the Master is also calling you into His service. Bring Him the fragments of your life — He will put them together again. An anointed message booklet .... #000702 $2.00

 THE MERCY SEAT. The Days of Grace are coming to a close, and the Days of Mercy are now here. And oh, how we need mercy! There never has been a time when we needed it more!.......................... #000711 $2.00

THROW THE HEAD OF SHEBA OVER THE WALL! David's enemy led an insurrection against him immediately following Absolom's revolt. A great mother in Israel intervened to put a stop to the uprising and saved her city from destruction. Will you take a stand? .... #000717 $2.00

CHILDREN'S BOOKS BY GWEN SHAW

LITTLE ONES TO HIM BELONG. Based on the testimonies of children's visions of Heaven and the death of a small Chinese boy, Sister Gwen weaves a delightful story of the precious joys of Heaven for children of all ages...................................#000901 $9.00

TELL ME THE STORIES OF JESUS. Some of the greatest New Testament stories of the Life of Jesus and written in a way that will interest children and help them to love Jesus...........#000902 $9.00

BOOKS ABOUT HEAVEN

INTRA MUROS — Rebecca Springer. One of the most beautiful books about Heaven is available here in its unabridged form. Read the glorious account of this ordinary believer's visit to Heaven. It brings great comfort to the bereaved......................................#109101 $8.00

PARADISE, THE HOLY CITY AND THE GLORY OF THE THRONE — Elwood Scott. Visited by a saint of God who spent forty days in Heaven, Elwood Scott's detailed description will edify and comfort your heart. Especially good for those with lost loved ones. Look into Heaven!...#104201 $8.00

PROPHECIES AND VISIONS

THE DAY OF THE LORD IS NEAR: Vol. I - IV. *"Surely the Lord GOD will do nothing, but he revealeth his secret unto his servants the prophets.""* (Amos 3:7) A collection of prophecies, visions and dreams. This startling compilation will help you understand what God has in His heart for the near future. ....Each Volume $10.00 • Volumes I - IV with binder..#001000 $25.00

BOOKS PUBLISHED BY ENGELTAL PRESS

ATTITUDES IN THE BEATITUDES — Esther Rollins. An instructor of the Word of God for 50 years, Esther taught this anointed course on the Beatitudes as a guest teacher at our School of Ministry. Both basic and profound, this dynamic teaching is full of insight for the Christian walk...#098801 $5.95

BANISHED FOR FAITH — Emil Waltner. The stirring story of the courageous forefathers of Gwen Shaw, the Hutterite Mennonites, who were banished from their homeland and suffered great persecution for their faith. Republished with an index and epilogue by Gwen Shaw. ....#126201 $12.95

BECOMING A SERVANT — Robert Baldwin. Learn what is on God's heart about servanthood. We must learn to serve before we can be trusted to lead. If you want to be great in God's Kingdom, learn to be the servant of all ....#006901 $2.00

FIVE STONES AND A SWORD — Gene Little. Read the true account of how Jesus is appearing to His lost children, and revealing Himself to these sons of Abraham. Your heart will leap with joy, and you will be encouraged, with new faith, that God will send a great revival among the Moslem people of the world ....#072501 #1.50

FOOTPRINTS — Larry Hunt. A collection of poems and stories reflecting the hand of God upon this humble pastor during 35 years of ministry..#057901 $3.75

FROM DUST TO GLORY — June Lewis. The Lord intends more than just salvation for us. He is making vessels of eternal Glory if we submit to Him. Rise up from your dust! ....#072001 $7.50

HOLY ANN — Helen Bingham. This humble Irish woman moved the arm of God through simple faith and prevailing prayer. Read these modern miracles that are told like a story from the Old Testament. The record of a lifetime of answered prayer...........................#010501 $4.95

IT WAS WORTH IT ALL — Elly Matz. The story of a beautiful woman whose courage will inspire you. Feel her heart as she tells of her starving father, the young Communist engineer she married, the villages mysteriously evacuated, the invading German army, the concentration camp where she was a prisoner, and her escape into freedom...#078001 $5.95

LET'S KEEP MOVING — Pete Snyder. Travel with Peter to Haiti where he struggles with the call of God to be a missionary. Identify with Peter's growth of faith through trials and tribulations as he travels on to China where new adventures await and faithful endurance is needed. A must for the called! ....#108801 $9.95

10

RULING IN THEIR MIDST — June Lewis. The Lord has called us to rule even in the midst of all demonic activity and Satan's plans and schemes. Sister June has learned spiritual warfare from the Lord Himself, *"who teacheth my hands to war,""* in the face of personal tragedy ....#072002 $6.00

Prices are subject to change.

For a complete catalogue with current pricing, contact:

Engeltal Press

P.O. Box 447
Jasper, ARK 72641 U.S.A.
Telephone (870) 446-2665
Fax (870) 446-2259
Email books@eth-s.org
Website www.engeltalpress.com